THE IMPORTANCE OF

Julius Caesar

These and other titles are included in The Importance
Of biography series:

Alexander the Great	Adolf Hitler
Muhammad Ali	Harry Houdini
Louis Armstrong	Thomas Jefferson
James Baldwin	Mother Jones
Clara Barton	Chief Joseph
Napoleon Bonaparte	Malcolm X
Julius Caesar	Margaret Mead
Rachel Carson	Michelangelo
Charlie Chaplin	Wolfgang Amadeus Mozart
Cesar Chavez	John Muir
Winston Churchill	Sir Isaac Newton
Cleopatra	Richard Nixon
Christopher Columbus	Georgia O'Keeffe
Hernando Cortes	Louis Pasteur
Marie Curie	Pablo Picasso
Amelia Earhart	Elvis Presley
Thomas Edison	Jackie Robinson
Albert Einstein	Norman Rockwell
Duke Ellington	Anwar Sadat
Dian Fossey	Margaret Sanger
Benjamin Franklin	Oskar Schindler
Galileo Galilei	John Steinbeck
Emma Goldman	Jim Thorpe
Jane Goodall	Mark Twain
Martha Graham	Queen Victoria
Stephen Hawking	Pancho Villa
Jim Henson	H. G. Wells

THE IMPORTANCE OF

Julius Caesar

by
Don Nardo

Lucent Books, P.O. Box 289011, San Diego, CA 92198-9011

Library of Congress Cataloging-in-Publication Data

Nardo, Don, 1947–
    The importance of Julius Caesar / by Don Nardo
        p. cm. — (The importance of)
    Includes bibliographical references and index.
    Summary: A biography of the Roman general and states-
man whose brilliant military leadership helped make Rome the
center of a vast empire.
    ISBN 1-56006-083-2 (alk. paper)
    1. Caesar, Julius—Influence—Juvenile literature.   2. Heads
of state—Rome—Biography—Juvenile literature.   3. Generals—Rome—Biography—Juvenile literature.   4. Rome—
History—Republic, 265–30 B.C.—Juvenile literature. [1. Caesar,
Julius. 2. Heads of state. 3. Generals. 4. Rome—History—
Republic, 265–30 B.C.] I. Title. II. Series.
DG261.N475   1997
937'.02'092—dc20   96-14186
[B]   CIP
                                                            AC

Copyright 1997 by Lucent Books, Inc., P.O. Box 289011,
San Diego, California, 92198-9011

Printed in the U.S.A.

Contents

Foreword

THE IMPORTANCE OF biography series deals with individuals who have made a unique contribution to history. The editors of the series have deliberately chosen to cast a wide net and include people from all fields of endeavor. Individuals from politics, music, art, literature, philosophy, science, sports, and religion are all represented. In addition, the editors did not restrict the series to individuals whose accomplishments have helped change the course of history. Of necessity, this criterion would have eliminated many whose contribution was great, though limited. Charles Darwin, for example, was responsible for radically altering the scientific view of the natural history of the world. His achievements continue to impact the study of science today. Others, such as Chief Joseph of the Nez Percé, played a pivotal role in the history of their own people. While Joseph's influence does not extend much beyond the Nez Percé, his nonviolent resistance to white expansion and his continuing role in protecting his tribe and his homeland remain an inspiration to all.

These biographies are more than factual chronicles. Each volume attempts to emphasize an individual's contributions both in his or her own time and for posterity. For example, the voyages of Christopher Columbus opened the way to European colonization of the New World. Unquestionably, his encounter with the New World brought monumental changes to both Europe and the Americas in his day. Today, however, the broader impact of Columbus's voyages is being critically scrutinized. *Christopher Columbus,* as well as every biography in The Importance Of series, includes and evaluates the most recent scholarship available on each subject.

Each author includes a wide variety of primary and secondary source quotations to document and substantiate his or her work. All quotes are footnoted to show readers exactly how and where biographers derive their information, as well as provide stepping stones to further research. These quotations enliven the text by giving readers eyewitness views of the life and times of each individual covered in The Importance Of series.

Finally, each volume is enhanced by photographs, bibliographies, chronologies, and comprehensive indexes. For both the casual reader and the student engaged in research, The Importance Of biographies will be a fascinating adventure into the lives of people who have helped shape humanity's past and present, and who will continue to shape its future.

Important Dates in the Life of Julius Caesar

B.C. 753
Traditional date for Rome's founding by Romulus, a descendent of the legendary hero Aeneas, from whom Caesar claimed his own family was descended.

509
A group of well-to-do Roman landowners throw out their king and establish the Roman Republic.

100
Caesar is born into an upper-class Roman family headed by his father, Gaius Julius Caesar, who names the boy after himself.

84
Caesar marries Cornelia, daughter of the popular politician Cornelius Cinna.

75
Caesar is captured by pirates near the Greek island of Rhodes; after paying a ransom to gain his freedom, he returns with troops, captures the pirates, and eventually executes them.

71
Marcus Crassus and Gnaeus Pompey, powerful figures who will later play important roles in Caesar's life, become national heroes by defeating a slave army led by the rebellious Spartacus.

69
Caesar attains the post of quaestor, or financial administrator, in which capacity he serves for a year in Spain.

65
Caesar is elected aedile, or overseer of public buildings, safety, and entertainment.

60
To oppose the Senate and gain power, Caesar, Crassus, and Pompey form an alliance later referred to as the First Triumvirate; Caesar wins the consulship for the following year.

58
Caesar assumes his proconsulship, or governorship, of the province of Narbonese Gaul, what is now southern France; he attacks and defeats the Helvetii tribe in central Gaul.

55–54
Caesar leads two brief and largely indecisive expeditions across the English Channel into southern Britain.

50
The Roman Senate calls for Caesar to surrender command of his army.

49
Caesar defies the Senate and at the head of his troops crosses the Rubicon River in northern Italy, initiating a Roman civil war.

48
Caesar delivers Pompey a shattering defeat at Pharsalus, in east-central Greece; Pompey flees to Egypt, where the local ruler, Ptolemy, has him murdered; Caesar meets Cleopatra, Ptolemy's sister, and backs her in a civil war against her brother.

47
Caesar defeats Ptolemy's forces and installs Cleopatra on Egypt's throne.

46
Caesar celebrates four magnificent triumphs for his victories in Gaul, Egypt, Pontus, and Africa.

45
Caesar orders a major revision of the Roman calendar, producing the "Julian" version that later becomes standard in the Western world.

44
Caesar becomes dictator *perpetuo*, or "for life"; a group of his enemies murders him in the Senate on the 15th, or Ides, of March; the conspirators flee Italy.

43
Caesar's immediate successors, Mark Antony, Marcus Lepidus, and Caesar's adopted son Octavian, form the Second Triumvirate.

27
After defeating his fellow triumvirs, Octavian becomes Augustus Caesar, first emperor of the Roman Empire, an autocratic state built largely on Caesar's blueprint for a benevolent dictatorship.

On a Quest for Ultimate Power

Over the centuries, the name Caesar, first made famous by the Roman general and politician Julius Caesar, has become synonymous with concepts of power and majesty. It was no accident that the modern nations of Germany and Russia originally chose the terms *Kaiser* and *Czar* respectively to designate their supreme leaders. Both titles are versions of the name Caesar. Likewise, military dictators and kings have sometimes been described as "acting like a Caesar" or as "modern Caesars." And politicians and army generals seen as ambitious or power-hungry are often compared to Caesar. For example, for his 1978 biography of General Douglas MacArthur, one of the United States' most ambitious and controversial military leaders, scholar William Manchester chose the title *American Caesar.*

Great literature, in recording Caesar's legendary deeds, has also emphasized his power and prestige. William Shakespeare's play *Julius Caesar,* written in 1599, is perhaps the most famous example. The author based his characters and plot on the writings of ancient Greek and Roman historians, especially Plutarch, Appian, and Suetonius. These writers lived and worked only a few years after Caesar's death and constantly emphasized how his bold seizing and exercising of power had

profoundly reshaped the social and political landscapes of Rome and its Mediterranean neighbors. Shakespeare skillfully conveyed this image of overwhelming power in the lines of the disgruntled Roman senator Cassius, who complains that Caesar

> Is now become a god, and Cassius is
> A wretched creature, and must bend his body [bow]
> If Caesar carelessly but nod on him. . . .
> Why man, he doth bestride [stand over] the narrow world
> Like a Colossus [giant statue], and we petty men
> Walk under his huge legs and peep about
> To find ourselves dishonorable graves.[1]

Similarly, the witty British playwright George Bernard Shaw captured Caesar's lofty ambition and supreme authority. In the opening of his delightful 1898 play *Caesar and Cleopatra,* Shaw also depicted the enormous arrogance that usually comes with such power. Caesar, on his famous visit to Egypt, stands before and addresses another symbol of power and majesty—the great Egyptian sphinx. "Hail Sphinx!" says Caesar:

More than most other noted historical leaders, the Roman politician and general Julius Caesar understood how to manipulate others to gain power.

In the little world yonder, Sphinx, my place is as high as yours in this great desert; only I wander, and you sit still; I conquer and you endure. . . . My way hither [to here] was the way of destiny; for I am he of whose genius you are the symbol: part brute, part woman, and part god—nothing of man in me at all.[2]

Such unflattering later depictions of Caesar as an ambitious, arrogant, and power-hungry individual might seem exaggerated and distorted by the passage of time and growth of his legend. And yet they were not. Indeed, Caesar was one of history's few great figures whose actual life was as dramatic and momentous as his later reputation. In his own day, he was without a doubt the most powerful and ambitious man in the strongest nation the

world had ever seen. He understood completely the dynamics of power, that is, how to manipulate Rome's military forces, government, and ruling class for his own political gain. And he cared little what laws he broke or who he hurt on his way to the top. Commenting on Caesar's ruthlessness, Suetonius wrote in *Lives of the Twelve Caesars*:

> Neither when in command of armies nor as a magistrate at Rome did he show an ethical integrity. . . . He pillaged shrines and temples of the gods filled with offerings [donations], and oftener sacked towns for the sake of plunder than for any fault . . . while later on he met the heavy expenses of the civil wars and his triumphs [victory parades] and entertainments by the most bare-faced pillage and sacrilege.[3]

Caesar held that such ruthless methods were absolutely necessary to achieve and maintain great power. In the long run, he firmly believed, whatever suffering he had to inflict was worth it to the state and to the people. For once in total control, he, the mighty and supremely wise Caesar, would transform society for its own good. Thus, like all dictators, he rationalized his own ambitions and harsh policies as being for the benefit of those he ruled. Unlike most other dictators who have dreamed of ruling the world, however, he managed to make his dream a reality. And that is why his life was a true reflection of his remarkable legendary image. The story of Julius Caesar, then, is that of a larger-than-life individual on a quest for ultimate power, of a man who coveted the world and for one brief, shining moment held it in his hands.

1 A Rising Star in Rome: Caesar's Early Years

On July 12, 100 B.C., Gaius Julius Caesar and his wife Aurelia announced the birth of a son. As was a common custom in Rome, they named the child after his father. The name Julius was derived from the family name of the Julii, who proudly traced their origins back through the mists of time to Julus, a son of the legendary hero Aeneas. According to tradition, Aeneas was a Trojan prince who escaped the ancient city of Troy, in Asia Minor, or what is now Turkey, when the Greeks burned it after a ten-year siege.

Aeneas sailed to Italy, where his descendent, Romulus, established the city of Rome in the year 753 B.C. Later, after reaching manhood, the younger Caesar would claim an even more illustrious lineage in order to bolster his public image. According to his biographer Ernle Bradford, Caesar

laid claim to an ancestry so ancient that it could not be disputed since there were no records except that on both sides his family had been noble

The legendary hero Aeneas, bearing his father Anchises on his back, flees the burning city of Troy. After many adventures, Aeneas will land in Italy, where his descendants will found the city of Rome.

Roman Family Values

The importance that Julius Caesar placed on his family's public image was typical of members of the Roman upper classes. So was his pre-occupation with the government and the military. This was because Roman society revolved around family status, and public service was the most accepted vehicle for elevating that status. In The Romans, 850 B.C.–A.D. 337, *historian Donald R. Dudley elaborates:*

"Almost all the literary evidence we have for [Roman] social life relates to the upper classes. Here a salient [striking] feature is the importance of the *gens* or clan. A man saw himself in terms of the *gens* of which he was a member, measuring his conduct by the standards of his ancestors (*maiores*), hoping by his own achievements to add to the glory of the *gens* and serve as an example to posterity. . . . Achievement was measured almost wholly in terms of public service in peace and war. No class in history can have been so devoted to politics as the nobility of the Republic. To hold office and especially the consulship, to lead armies to victory, to command respect in the Senate, were the objects which generation after generation [strove for]. . . . With these values, the Roman nobility was conservative and backward looking, admiring conformity rather than originality in an individual. . . . Private life was centered on the family—the natural biological unit of the husband, wife, and unmarried children, together with the slaves . . . who lived with them under the same roof. Within it, law and custom vested an absolute authority in the father (*paterfamilias*). He had control of the family property and . . . [the] powers of life and death over its members."

since time immemorial. In one public speech he was to declare that his family were descended in direct line from Venus/Aphrodite (goddess of love). Since . . . the goddess was the mother of Aeneas . . . the founder of the Roman race, Caesar was laying claim to an ancestry that could not be challenged. His admirers seemed to have accepted this explanation of his lineage, although how much Caesar himself believed it must remain doubtful.[4]

The name Caesar was the cognomen, or surname, denoting a specific branch of the Julii family, the one that included Caesar's immediate ancestors and himself.

Strong Family Ties

The parents of the child who would one day become one of the greatest military generals and statesmen of all time belonged to the patrician class. The patricians, or wealthy landowners, made up Roman society's ancient and prestigious aristocracy. Rome, like most other ancient lands, had originally been ruled by kings. But in 509 B.C., a group of leading patricians threw out their king and established the Roman Republic.

In the early republic, citizens, at the time only adult males born of Roman families, met in a legislative body called the Assembly. Because most members were also patricians, many of the common people—the plebeians, or plebes—objected. So the government soon established a second body, the Popular Assembly, from which patricians were excluded. Both assemblies voted on new laws and chose leaders, the most important of these being the two consuls, who together served a one-year term, and whose duties were to administer the state and lead the armies. Another legislative body, the elite Senate, was composed strictly of patricians. The senators formulated much local and foreign state policy. More importantly, they closely advised the consuls, and, using their money and position, influenced the way citizens voted in the assemblies. Thus, the real power in the republic lay in the patrician Senate, whose ranks included many former consuls and other state officials.

Young Julius Caesar's family had its own modest share of prestigious officials. When the boy was eight, in 92 B.C., his father was chosen to be a praetor. Second in rank only to the consuls, the two annually elected praetors were charged with seeing that justice, including the administration of the laws and courts, was carried out. A year later, when his praetorship ended, the elder Caesar became proconsul, or

governor, of the Roman province of Asia, which then encompassed western Asia Minor. Also in the year 91, Caesar's uncle, Sextus Julius Caesar, was elected consul.

In addition, Caesar had strong family ties with some of the most powerful men of his day, and these relationships constitute what little is known of his youthful years. First, his father's sister Julia married the powerful army general Gaius Marius. A man of towering reputation, Marius had been elected consul seven times. In this capacity he commanded the vast Roman military machine that had, under his predecessors, conquered much of the known world in the prior few centuries.

Rome's conquests had begun in the 400s B.C. Marching outward from the city,

Gaius Marius, Caesar's uncle, was elected to the powerful office of consul seven times.

which was located along the Tiber River in the fertile plain of Latium in west-central Italy, Roman armies relentlessly attacked and subdued neighboring Italian tribes and peoples. By 265 Rome had managed to unify all of Italy south of the Po Valley, located in the north near the Alps mountain range. In the following century and a half, the Romans absorbed the Po Valley, which they called Cisalpine Gaul, and also won three devastating wars with Carthage, an empire centered in what is now Tunisia in northern Africa. The Carthaginian homeland eventually became the Roman province of Africa. Also during this period, Rome turned eastward and seized control of the Greek-ruled kingdoms of Macedonia, Seleucia, and Egypt. By the time Marius came to power seven years before Caesar's birth, the Mediterranean Sea had become, in effect, a Roman lake.

The New Military Reality

Marius himself helped to maintain Rome's iron grip over the Mediterranean world by vanquishing a dangerous uprising in Africa in 107 B.C. Two years later, he stopped the Cimbri and Teutones, semi-civilized tribes from central Europe, from overrunning the Roman provinces of Spain, Cisalpine Gaul, and Narbonese Gaul, or what is now southern France. But Marius's most important and lasting accomplishment was his revision of the military and its recruitment system. As historian Lily Ross Taylor explains in her book *Party Politics in the Age of Caesar*:

> It was Marius who introduced the personal army as a decisive factor in Roman politics. Before his day the Roman soldier had in general been recruited from the small landholders of Roman territory, but the normal levies failed after the supply of these landholders had been depleted by Rome's long and costly wars. To find the troops he needed . . . Marius turned for recruits to the landless poor, the proletariat [laboring class] of Rome and the Italian [townships]. He raised an army of soldiers ready to serve under him in the hope of personal gain, that is, the acquisition of a land bonus. During the war with the Cimbri and Teutones . . . the number of his soldiers grew steadily. When in 100 B.C. he was consul for the sixth time, Marius had a large band of trained soldiers and veterans who owed allegiance to him and looked to him for rewards.[5]

Thus began a trend in which soldiers felt more of a sense of loyalty to their generals than to the state. Caesar himself would eventually take full advantage of this new military reality, which would steadily weaken the republic's central authority.

As a boy, Caesar no doubt witnessed or heard firsthand about his uncle Marius's dealings, both military and political. Partly because of his acceptance of landless plebes for military service, and also because he himself had been born a commoner, Marius became the leader of the *populares*, a political party that promoted the rights of everyday people. Opposing the *populares* were the *optimates*, a party made up mainly of senators and other upper-class patricians. The *optimates* advocated that control of the state should remain in the hands of Rome's "best men,"

A likeness of Cornelius Sulla, who declared himself dictator of Rome after defeating Marius's forces in a brief but bloody civil war.

The Work of Butchery

To their surprise, however, the leading *populares*, including Caesar, soon found that they had sorely underestimated Sulla's abilities and determination. In 83 B.C. Sulla returned from the east and marched his battle-hardened army on Rome, igniting a brief but bloody civil war. Sulla's forces won, and he achieved his revenge on Marius by killing thousands of *populares*. As Plutarch described it in his *Life of Sulla*:

> Sulla now devoted himself entirely to the work of butchery. The city was filled with murder and there was no counting the executions or setting a limit to them. Many people were killed because of purely personal ill feeling; they had no connection with Sulla in any way, but Sulla, in order to gratify members of his own party, permitted them to be done away with. . . . Then immediately . . . Sulla published a list of eighty men to be condemned. Public opinion was horrified, but, after a single day's interval, he published another list containing 220 more names, and next day a third list with the same number of names on it. . . . He also condemned anyone who sheltered or attempted to save a person whose name was on the lists. Death was the penalty for such acts of humanity.[6]

The following year Sulla made himself dictator. The office of dictator was a seldom-used institution in which the government appointed a trusted individual to save the state in a national emergency. A dictator had complete authority over the country

namely themselves. In 88 one of Marius's former assistants, Cornelius Sulla, became consul and switched sides. As Sulla assumed leadership of the *optimates*, the relations between the two political groups became strained, and violent confrontation seemed imminent.

That dreaded confrontation came after Sulla left Rome to put down a rebellion in Asia Minor. In his absence, Marius immediately seized the opportunity and murdered many of Sulla's supporters, putting the *populares* in power. The young Caesar supported his uncle in this endeavor. When Marius died suddenly in 86, Caesar sought a means to retain his prominent position in the *populares*. Two years later, the sixteen-year-old Caesar found a way to do so by marrying Cornelia, daughter of Cornelius Cinna, the new leader of the popular party.

Roman versus Roman in a massive bloodbath as Sulla and his soldiers seize control of the Roman capital.

but had to step down after a term of six months. However Sulla, by brute force, made the term of his rule indefinite. For three more years he held the power of life and death in Rome and continued to exercise that power over his opponents.

For reasons that remain unclear, during this bloody purge Sulla at first chose to spare Caesar. Perhaps the dictator recognized the young man's brilliant mind and thought he could benefit from having Caesar join and support the *optimates.* In any case Sulla summoned Caesar and demanded that he divorce Cornelia as a symbolic way of renouncing his allegiance to the *populares.* Caesar boldly refused and then went into hiding in order to escape

Sulla's wrath. In the meantime, Caesar's relatives begged Sulla to forgive the young man, insisting that he was just high-spirited and certainly guiltless of any crime. The dictator eventually gave in and granted Caesar his life, on the condition that the family keep the boy out of his sight. Sulla, who had looked Caesar in the eye and recognized a potentially dangerous opponent, gave Caesar's kin a warning that would one day prove correct: "Bear in mind that the man you are so eager to save will one day deal the death blow to the cause of the [Roman] aristocracy, which you have joined with me in upholding; for in this Caesar there is more than one Marius."[7]

Making a Favorable Impression

To make sure that Caesar remained safe from Sulla, the Julii used their influence to secure him a post far from Rome. In 81 B.C. the young man journeyed to the province of Asia to work on the staff of the local governor, Minucius Thermus. Caesar's first mission was as a diplomat to the nearby kingdom of Bithynia, a Roman ally located along the southern shore of the Black Sea. He and the king, Nicomedes IV, took a liking to each other and remained friends for many years. About a year after meeting Nicomedes, Caesar saw his first military action when he helped Thermus storm a rebellious island town. Nothing specific is known of Caesar's exploits in this incident, but he apparently distinguished himself. Afterward, in a solemn ceremony, the governor decorated the twenty-year-old with the *corona civica*, or civic crown, an award given for saving the life of a fellow soldier in battle.

While still in Asia Minor in 78, Caesar received the stunning news that Sulla had died. It was now safe for the young man to return to Rome, and he did so almost immediately. With Sulla gone, the senators and consuls had retaken control of the city and empire, and political tensions had eased considerably. Caesar reasoned that the situation was now ripe for him to begin making a political name for himself. And the best way to do that seemed to be to exploit his extraordinary talent for public speaking. Very soon after returning home, Caesar volunteered to prosecute two of Sulla's most prominent supporters, who stood accused of growing rich at the public's expense during the recent dicta-

torship. Caesar was exercising the right of any Roman citizen to come forward, make an accusation of wrongdoing, and prosecute the case in court.

Caesar had made a wise move, for his public performance instantly made a favorable impression on many members of the ruling class. Part of this impression was due to his imposing physical attributes. He was, wrote Suetonius,

> tall of stature, with a fair complexion, shapely limbs, a somewhat full face, and keen black eyes. . . . He was somewhat overnice in the care of his person, being not only carefully trimmed and shaved, but even having unwanted facial hairs plucked out. . . . They say,

According to the ancient Roman writer Suetonius, Julius Caesar (below) was a tall, imposing, and extremely well groomed individual.

too, that he was fantastic in his dress; that he wore a senator's tunic with fringed sleeves reaching to the wrist, and always had a girdle [wide belt] over it, though rather a loose one.[8]

Caesar's forceful oratory made an even stronger impression. He spoke in a high-pitched voice filled with emotion and used grand gestures and facial expressions to dramatize his points. "In Rome," Plutarch recorded in his *Life of Caesar*, "Caesar won a brilliant reputation and great popularity by his eloquence [persuasive ability] at these trials."[9]

Indeed, Caesar made sure to be just as friendly and persuasive in his everyday dealings with people. He often threw lavish parties and did favors for associates and acquaintances, calculating correctly

---

Caesar's Compassionate Side

Although Caesar was doubtless a ruthless man who frequently used underhanded and brutal tactics against his opponents, he apparently had a warmer, more compassionate side. In this excerpt from his Lives of the Twelve Caesars, *the Roman historian Suetonius recorded some of Caesar's better known acts of friendship and mercy.*

"His friends he treated with invariable kindness and consideration. When Gaius Oppius [one of his military assistants] was his companion on a journey through a wild, woody country and was suddenly taken ill, Caesar gave up to him the only shelter there was, while he himself slept on the ground out-of-doors. Moreover, when he came to power, he advanced some of his friends to the highest positions, even though they were of the humblest origin, and when taken to task for it [by his political opponents], flatly declared that if he had been helped in defending his honor by brigands and cut-throats, he would have rewarded such men in the same way. . . . Even when avenging wrongs he was by nature most merciful, and when he got hold of the pirates who had captured him, he had them crucified, since he had sworn beforehand that he would do so, but ordered that their throats be cut first [to spare them the agony of a long death on the cross]. . . . When summoned as a witness against Publius Clodius [his wife Pompeia's lover, who had been caught wearing female attire in her bedchamber], Caesar declared that he had no evidence, although both his mother Aurelia and sister Julia had given the jurors a faithful account of the whole affair. . . . 'I maintain that the members of my family [Caesar declared] should be free from suspicion, as well as from guilt.'"

---

that this was the way to build a strong political reputation. Plutarch continued:

> He had an ability to make himself liked which was remarkable in one of his age, and he was very much in the good graces of the ordinary citizen because of his easy manners and the friendly way in which he mixed with people. Then there were his dinner parties and entertainments and a certain splendor about his whole way of life; all this made him gradually more and more important politically.[10]

Inevitable Opponents

Though he had proved himself an able public speaker, Caesar hoped to become an even better one. He, like so many other ambitious young patricians, wanted to be as brilliant a speaker as Marcus Tullius Cicero. Six years older than Caesar, Cicero, a patrician and affirmed member of the *optimates*, and like Caesar a rising star in Roman politics, had already made a name for himself as an orator without peer. In 76 B.C. Cicero won election to the post of quaestor, one of Rome's twenty financial administrators. Holding such high office automatically made him a candidate for the Senate, whose members served for life. Cicero became a senator in 74, and he quickly became a champion of the republican system, attempting to preserve its laws and traditions against the threats of ambitious and power-hungry men. Because Caesar was just such a man, he and Cicero inevitably became political opponents. Yet each grudgingly respected the other's formidable abilities. Thus, while

The great politician and orator Marcus Tullius Cicero delivers an impassioned speech to a crowd in the Roman forum.

he disagreed with Cicero's politics, Caesar admired and envied his adversary's speaking prowess.

In 75, when Cicero was still a quaestor, Caesar decided to travel to the island of Rhodes, off the coast of Asia Minor, to study oratory with the famous Greek orator Apollonius Molo. On the journey, Caesar fell prey to pirates, a menace that at the time was becoming increasingly dangerous throughout the Mediterranean. From numerous island strongholds, these brigands, expert sailors with swift ships, raided cargo vessels, farms, villas, and whole towns. They stole, raped, and killed at will. When a band of pirates captured Caesar's ship, they reasoned that this noble Roman would fetch a handsome ransom. Plutarch wrote:

> First, when the pirates demanded a ransom of twenty talents [one talent was roughly equivalent to $5,000 to $10,000 in today's money], Caesar burst out laughing. They did not know, he said, who it was that they had captured, and he volunteered to pay fifty.[11]

The conceited and apparently fearless young Roman remained the pirates' prisoner for thirty-eight days. During that time, he treated them as inferiors, often calling them illiterate savages and demanding that they keep quiet while he was napping. Impressed by his boldness, intellect, and keen sense of humor, the pirates put up with his arrogance. At one point Caesar promised his captors that when he gained release he would return and execute all of them. The pirates took this as a jest or idle boast, which proved to be a fatal mistake on their part. When Caesar's servants finally arrived with the money and his captors freed him, he immediately gathered a force of Roman troops and returned to the pirate stronghold. He easily overwhelmed and captured the brigands, then turned them over to the new governor of Asia. When that official failed to punish the criminals, Caesar seized and publicly crucified them, thus fulfilling his promise. His daring and decisiveness in this episode helped to establish his reputation as a formidable foe.

The valiant slave leader Spartacus dies in his final battle against the Romans, commanded on this occasion by the ambitious Crassus and Pompey.

In Crassus's and Pompey's Shadows

Upon returning to Rome, Caesar was determined to continue building that reputation, perhaps by securing some kind of military post or assignment. In Roman society, taking part in a successful military campaign was a sure way to gain fame, respect, and higher office. However he, along with other ambitious young men, now found himself in the shadows of two extraordinarily influential figures. They were Marcus Crassus and Gnaeus Pompey. Crassus was the wealthiest man in Rome, having made his fortune from silver mines and real estate ventures. Pompey was an accomplished general who had distinguished himself by winning battles against rebels in Spain.

Both men desired to further their reputations, and their chance came in 73 B.C. when a slave named Spartacus escaped from a gladiator school and led a large-scale rebellion that threatened the security of most of Italy. In 71 Crassus, with a last-minute assist from Pompey, defeated Spartacus's slave army, some ninety thousand strong, a feat that made the two men the national heroes of the moment. The following year they easily won election as consuls.

Caesar, now thirty, reasoned that for the foreseeable future Crassus and Pompey would continue to dominate Roman politics and the national spotlight. That forecast proved correct, especially for Pompey. In 67 the government assigned him a task of monumental difficulty and importance—to rid the seaways of the pirate menace, now a serious threat to national security. According to historian James Henry Breasted, the pirates

had overrun the whole Mediterranean. They even appeared at the mouth of the Tiber, robbing and burning. They kidnapped Roman officials on the Appian Way [the main road to and from Rome], but a few miles from Rome, and they finally captured the grain supplies coming into Rome from Egypt and Africa. . . . The Assembly of the people passed a law giving Pompey supreme command of the Mediterranean and for fifty miles back from its

---

Pompey's Audacity

Pompey's renowned courage and stubbornness are well illustrated in this tract from Plutarch's Life of Pompey, *part of the ancient biographer's larger work,* Lives of the Noble Grecians and Romans. *After defeating some of Sulla's enemies, Pompey asked Sulla for a triumph, or victory parade, however:*

"The request was opposed by Sulla who had pointed out that legally this was an honor which could be given to a consul or praetor, but to no one else. . . . And if Pompey, who had scarcely grown a beard as yet, and was too young even to be a senator, were to ride into Rome in a triumphal procession, people would be angry not only with Sulla's government but also with Pompey himself for receiving such an honor. Therefore, so Sulla said to Pompey, his request could not be allowed and he would oppose him and put a stop to his ambitious plans if he refused to give way. Pompey, however, was not in the least frightened. He asked Sulla to bear in mind the fact that more people worshipped the rising than the setting sun, implying that while his own power was on the increase, that of Sulla was growing less and less. Sulla . . . was astounded at Pompey's audacity and cried out twice in succession: 'Let him have his triumph!'"

shores. He was assigned two hundred ships and allowed to make his army as large as he thought necessary. No Roman commander had ever before held such far-reaching and unrepublican power.[12]

Giving one commander such unlimited power worried many Roman leaders, especially conservative republicans like Cicero. He saw the trend begun by Marius and Sulla, that of military strongmen holding too much power, as dangerous to the republic's stability. But at least in this instance Pompey did not abuse the great power the state had given him. In a lightning campaign of only forty days, he swept the seas of pirates, destroying their strongholds and sinking or capturing over seventeen hundred of their ships, all without losing a single Roman ship. This incredible achievement made Pompey a national hero of epic proportions.

Up the Political Ladder

Unlike Cicero, Caesar admired men like Pompey who wielded military power on a grand scale. More interested in his own welfare and glory than that of the state, Caesar wanted to match and even surpass the deeds of Pompey and Crassus. But Caesar was realistic enough to know that he was not yet in a position to compete with such men. The younger man lacked the military experience and glory, as well as the large sums of money needed to campaign for high offices, especially praetor and consul. Plenty of money was also necessary to bribe public officials and other influential individuals for career-advancing favors, a common practice in Roman politics.

So Caesar wisely set a goal of climbing the political ladder one step at a time. And all the while, he would amass as much money as possible until eventually he could realistically play in the same league with Crassus and Pompey. Caesar took two important first steps in his plan even before Pompey's triumph over the pirates. In 69 B.C., Caesar managed to gain a post as a quaestor in Spain. The job bored him, but he dutifully put in his time. When he returned to Rome the following year, he married Pompeia, an aristocratic young woman from the family of the former dictator, Sulla. Caesar's first wife, Cornelia, whom over the years he had grown to love, had died suddenly in

A bust of Gnaeus Pompey, who gained fame and glory fighting rebellious slaves in the 70s B.C. and ridding the Mediterranean of pirates in the decade that followed.

Wild Beasts and Gladiators

In his Lives of the Twelve Caesars, *Suetonius gives this account of Caesar's accomplishments as aedile, overseer of public buildings and entertainments, an office he assumed in 65 B.C.:*

"When aedile, Caesar decorated not only the Comitium [meeting place of the people's Assembly] and the Forum [main square] with its adjacent basilicas [public meeting areas], but the Capitol [hilltop dominated by temples and shrines] as well, building temporary colonnades [column-lined areas] for the display of a part of his programs. He exhibited combats with wild beasts and stage-plays too, both with his colleague [the other city aedile] and independently. The result was that Caesar alone took all the credit even for what they had spent in common. . . . Caesar gave a gladiatorial show besides but with somewhat fewer pairs of combatants than he had purposed; for the huge band [of trained warriors] which he had assembled from all quarters so terrified his [political] opponents, that a bill [law] was passed limiting the number of gladiators which anyone was to be allowed to keep in the city."

70. She left in his charge their young daughter Julia, about whom almost nothing is known. What is more certain is that after losing Cornelia, he no longer concerned himself with marriage's emotional aspects. This new union with Pompeia was strictly one of convenience. The cold fact was that Caesar needed money to finance his drive for power, and Pompeia's family was one of the richest in Rome.

Caesar put the extra money to good use in his next public post. With the help of the influential Crassus, with whom he had shrewdly become friendly, in 65 he gained the office of aedile. These officials were charged with maintaining public buildings and overseeing large-scale entertainments for the populace. Caesar outdid himself in this post, staging the most spectacular gladiatorial fights and wild beast hunts the city had ever witnessed. Gambling that it would help to increase his popularity, he even spent some of his own money on these events. That gamble paid off, for he became a household name. Now he felt ready to tackle a more formidable challenge—the office of praetor. He reasoned correctly that his tenure in this post would establish him at last as a major player in the game of national politics, although the dramatic way this would happen would surprise even him.

2 To the Summit of Power: Caesar Wins the Consulship

The five years following Caesar's decision to run for the office of praetor in the July 63 B.C. elections were for him both turbulent and eventful. This was the period in which he at last realized his dream of becoming a major player in Roman politics. Shortly after winning the praetorship, he shrewdly used an unexpected government crisis to gain further national recognition and then went on to win two other prestigious offices, including the consulship.

For Caesar, however, simply winning this lofty position and effectively serving his country was not enough. He wanted to take advantage of the high authority and national exposure that went with the position in order to enhance his own reputation and influence. Thereafter, he reasoned, he would be so formidable a political figure that he could assume other powerful positions at will and remain a guiding force in national affairs.

Working toward this goal, Caesar began to display the strong tactical skills that would characterize his later political and military maneuvers. He showed that he was capable of courting popular support from the masses and at the same time of making the backroom deals necessary to win over the rich and powerful. In the latter case, this meant dealing with Crassus and Pompey. Caesar was well aware that the influence these towering figures wielded constituted a significant obstacle in the path of any ambitious politician. Working with, rather than against, these men, he decided, would help to clear his way to the summit of state power.

Catiline's Conspiracy

On his upward journey toward that summit, Caesar had dutifully served in a number of increasingly important public offices, including quaestor and aedile. Most ambitious men seeking the consulship first served a year as praetor, and Caesar saw that it would be of benefit to him to follow that tradition. In addition to overseeing justice, the praetors performed some of the consular duties when the consuls themselves could not. And the prevailing custom was to reward a praetor at the end of his term by appointing him governor of a province. Caesar knew full well that many of Rome's past great men had significantly increased their reputations and personal fortunes while serving as provincial governors. Therefore, he approached the 63 B.C. elections, in which the people chose leaders for the following year, with considerable eagerness.

Caesar easily won the praetorship. But the results of the consular race soon brought about an unexpected national crisis that served to increase his public prominence even more. Caesar and Crassus both openly supported Lucius Sergius Catilina, popularly known as Catiline, for the office of consul. Catiline was a debt-ridden aristocrat with a reputation for shady dealings. But he ran his campaign as a *populare*. Caesar and Crassus, still firmly opposed to the *optimates*, hoped to benefit from his favors after he was elected. The *optimates*' chief spokesman, the great orator and republican champion Cicero, had easily defeated Catiline for the consulship the year before. So it came as no surprise to most people when Cicero, serving as consul in 63, used his own influence to help the *optimates* hand Catiline his second defeat.

However, Catiline, who had hoped that once in office he could somehow ma-nipulate his consular powers to erase his debts, became desperate in his loss. Seeking revenge against both Cicero and the state, he hatched a plan to kill the consuls and several other officials, burn part of the city, and then take over the government. To carry out this daring scheme, he secretly enlisted the aid of some other disgruntled noblemen and also assembled a small army composed of various disreputable individuals. In James Breasted's words, they were "the dissatisfied bankrupts, landless peasants, Sulla's veterans, outlaws, and slaves—the debased and lawless elements of Italy seeking an opportunity to rid themselves of debt or to better their situation."[13]

But in a city filled with political spies and opportunists, it was almost impossible to keep secret such a large-scale operation involving so many people. Caesar and Crassus quickly got wind of what Catiline was up to. Though they had supported

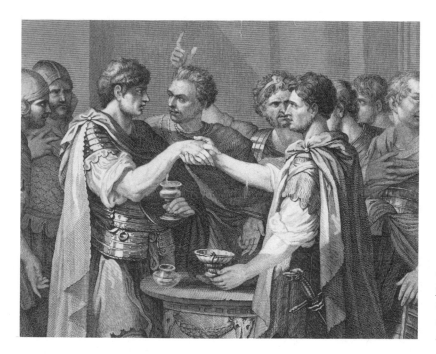

Catiline and his fellow conspirators seal their deadly pact, vowing to kill the consuls, including Cicero, and to seize control of the Roman government.

him before, they now worried about their own reputations and futures and prudently distanced themselves from him. Some evidence suggests that they were so eager to do so that they even informed their political enemy Cicero of the plot. In any case Cicero did find out and immediately swung into action. He gathered secret letters proving Catiline's guilt and exposed the conspiracy in a series of magnificent speeches to the Senate. According to Plutarch, Catiline attended one senatorial meeting, hoping to defend himself.

No senator, however, would sit near him; they all moved away from the bench where he was sitting. When he began to speak he was shouted down, and finally Cicero rose up and told him to leave the city. He himself, he said, was a statesman who achieved his results by words, whereas Catiline's method was armed force; it was only right, therefore, that they should be separated from each other by the city wall.[14]

People Remember Only What Happens Last

Soon afterward, Catiline fled the city and prepared his army of malcontents for a march on Rome. Meanwhile, Cicero rounded up the other leading conspira-

Cicero stands before his fellow legislators in the Senate House and denounces Catiline, who sits alone, shunned by the others, at lower right.

The Conspirators' Appalling Plans

Catiline's infamous conspiracy to overthrow the Roman government included a number of well-known patricians from respected families. In this excerpt from his Life of Cicero, *Plutarch describes one of these men and the appalling plans he and Catiline had for their enemies in Rome:*

"The remains of Catiline's corrupt crew who had been left behind in Rome [after Catiline fled the city] were organized and encouraged by Cornelius Lentulus, surnamed Sura. Lentulus came from a distinguished family, but had lived a low life and had once been expelled from the Senate for his debauched [corrupt] conduct. He was now serving as praetor for the second time, the normal procedure for those who have regained senatorial rank. . . . There was nothing . . . on a small scale or trivial about Lentulus's plans. In fact he had decided to kill the entire Senate and as many other citizens as possible, to burn down the city itself, and to spare no one except the children of Pompey. These were to be seized by the conspirators and held as hostages to secure a peaceful settlement with Pompey. . . . The conspirators, however, were unbalanced characters who seldom met together without wine and women, while Cicero [having been informed of the plot] was following their schemes with patient care, with sober judgment, and with exceptional intelligence. He had many agents outside the conspiracy who kept a close watch on what was going on and helped him to collect evidence. . . . [After Cicero presented this evidence to the Senate], Lentulus was arrested. He . . . laid aside his purple-bordered robe [senator's attire] in the Senate, and put on other clothes more in keeping with his present circumstances. He and his associates were then handed over to the praetors to be kept prisoner, though without chains."

tors. On December 5, 63 B.C., the Senate held a meeting to decide their fate. This meeting was a momentous one, for although no one realized it at the time, its results would also help to decide Cicero's and Caesar's fates. Cicero and several other senators advocated that the conspirators immediately, and without benefit of a trial, receive the death penalty. Then Caesar asked for permission to speak. Using all of his abilities as orator, he forcefully called for a sentence of life imprisonment instead. Under Roman law, he said, a person accused of a crime was entitled to a trial. And for the crime of plotting, rather than actually carrying out, a rebellion, the traditional sentence was usually life in prison. To go against tradition now, in the heat of anger, he warned, might only hurt the senators' own images later. "You," Caesar declared loudly,

> Fathers of the Senate, must beware of letting the guilt of [the conspirators] have more weight with you than your own dignity, and of taking more thought for your anger than for your good name. . . . I should advise limiting ourselves to such penalties as the law has established. . . . Do I then recommend that the prisoners be allowed to depart and swell Catiline's forces? By no means! This rather is my advice: that their goods be confiscated and that they themselves be kept imprisoned.[15]

Caesar warned that people "remember only that which happens last," meaning that after the conspirators' deeds were forgotten, Romans would remember only the senators' rash and harsh judgment.

For a moment, it seemed that Caesar had swayed many senators. But then Marcus Cato, a conservative member of the *optimates* who hated Caesar and other ambitious *populares*, rose and vehemently demanded that the prisoners be executed. Over Caesar's continued objections, the Senate agreed with Cato. Cicero immediately had the conspirators strangled in the city prison. For the time being, this action, along with the defeat of Catiline's army by republican forces a few months later, greatly enhanced Cicero's reputation. Many called him the republic's savior. But

just as Caesar had predicted, popular opinion soon began to turn against the Senate's harsh action. As a number of important public officials spoke out against the executions, Caesar gained the image of a wise and merciful leader who had had the courage to oppose the Senate's abuse of established law and tradition.

The Catiline episode made Caesar more popular than ever with both the plebes and more well-to-do *populares*, all of whom wanted to see the Senate's power curbed. It is important to note, however, that ambitious men like Caesar and Crassus were not and never had been true *populares*. Their purported sympathy for the common people and respect for the law, as illustrated by Caesar's speech to the senators, was merely a ploy, a means of garnering popular support for advancing their own political goals. By embracing the *populares*' cause, Caesar had a convenient platform from which to oppose the *optimates* and the Senate. The Catiline affair taught him two important lessons about what methods to use against these opponents. He realized, historian F. R. Cowell points out, "that he could not get the influence he wanted in the government of Rome by the indirect method of having a nominee elected as consul. He must also have lost any illusions he may have had upon the ease and safety with which power could be won by revolution and armed rebellion."[16]

✳ Snubbed by the Senate

Caesar soon learned another important political lesson, this time from Pompey, who had been away on a military campaign in Asia Minor. Late in 62 B.C. word

Cato Demands the Death Penalty

After Caesar delivered his impassioned speech calling for life imprisonment rather than the death penalty for the Catilinian conspirators, Cato, a conservative senator, spoke in rebuttal. In his historical chronicle The War with Catiline, *the Roman historian Sallust recorded Cato as saying:*

"My feelings are very different [from those of Caesar], Fathers of the Senate, when I turn my mind to the plot and the danger we are in, and when I reflect upon the recommendations of some of our number. The speakers appear to me to have dwelt upon the punishment of these men who have plotted warfare on their country, parents, altars, and hearths; but the situation warns us rather to take precautions against them than to argue about what we are to do with them. . . . Nay, in the name of the immortal gods I call upon you, who have always valued your houses, villas, statues, and paintings more highly than your own country; if you wish to retain the treasures to which you cling . . . if you even wish to provide peace for the enjoyment of your pleasures, wake up at last and lay hold of the reins of the state. Here is no question of revenues or the wrongs of our allies; our lives and liberties are at stake. . . . In fine and finished phrases did Gaius [Julius] Caesar a moment ago before this body speak of life and death. . . . He recommended that the goods of the prisoners be confiscated, and that they themselves be imprisoned. . . . This advice is utterly futile if Caesar fears danger from the conspirators; but if amid such general fear he alone has none, I have the more reason to fear for you and for myself. Be assured, then, that when you decide the fate of Lentulus [Catiline's fellow conspirator] and the rest, you will at the same time be passing judgment on Catiline's army and all the conspirators. . . . This, then, is my recommendation: whereas our country has been subjected to the greatest peril through the abominable plot of wicked citizens . . . [who] have confessed that they have planned murder, arson, and other fearful and cruel crimes against their fellow citizens and their country, let those who have confessed . . . be punished [with the ultimate penalty]."

came that Pompey was returning to Rome. Remembering Sulla's fateful and brutal return from the east, many people, including Caesar and Crassus, feared that Pompey would march his huge army on Rome. As Plutarch wrote:

Rumors of every kind were scattered abroad about Pompey . . . so that there was a great commotion [in Rome], as if he intended to march with his army into the city and establish himself as sole ruler. Crassus withdrew himself,

Pompey, surrounded by his chief military aides, rides in his triumph, or victory parade, after sweeping the seas of the pirate menace.

together with his children and property, out of the city.[17]

However, Pompey surprised everyone by disbanding his army and appearing in Rome with only a handful of followers. By passing up his chance to be a self-appointed dictator like Sulla, Pompey shrewdly cemented his already widespread support among the common people. To be sure, he was no more a true *populare* than either Caesar or Crassus. Like his two most important rivals, Pompey intended to manipulate the *populares* for his own selfish motives. Disbanding his army was also intended to increase his prestige and influence among the senators, whom he expected to show him gratitude for refraining from violence. However, this trick did not work, a fact that Caesar never forgot. F. R. Cowell explains:

Pompey was the last great Roman commander of the Republic voluntarily to renounce supreme power. His example merely proved to others, particularly to Julius Caesar, what a fool he had been. The behavior of the Senate showed little gratitude for, or understanding of, Pompey's undoubtedly great achievements. . . . So badly did the senators behave that Pompey himself must have realized the folly of his self-denial. For the senators would not, as he asked . . . provide land settlements for his demobilized soldiers.[18]

Not long after they arrogantly refused Pompey his land bill, the senators snubbed Caesar, too. Early in 61 Caesar, now thirty-nine, left for Farther (southwestern) Spain, the province he had been granted at the conclusion of his praetorship. There, he found himself in command of about ten thousand troops. After raising another five thousand, he launched a small but successful campaign against some fierce hill tribes who had been harassing the local inhabitants. When his one-year term as governor was up, and he arrived back in Rome in 60, Caesar expected the Senate to accord him a triumph, the usual reward for victorious returning commanders. But the senators, urged on by his enemy Cato, who knew Caesar had his sights on a consulship, claimed that Caesar could not have a triumph and run for consul, too. He would have to choose one or the other. Caesar chose the latter.

The First Triumvirate

The *optimates'* shabby treatment of both Pompey and Caesar had been designed to keep these ambitious men in their place, weaken the *populares*, and assert senatorial authority. But the plan backfired. No one had expected Caesar and Pompey, respectful but staunch rivals, to join forces, but this they did. Sometime in the summer of 60 B.C., probably shortly before the consular elections, Caesar engineered a secret alliance with Pompey and then approached Crassus, too. Crassus made no bones about his dislike for Pompey and likely also envied and feared Caesar's obvious abilities and ambitions. But Crassus had also recently been rebuffed by the Senate, which had helped to defeat a financial bill he had proposed. Singly, each of the three men lacked the resources to overshadow the Senate, but by combining their wealth and influence, Caesar proposed, they could conceivably manipulate the government to their own ends. And so

A meeting of the members of the powerful political partnership, the First Triumvirate—Gnaeus Pompey, Julius Caesar, and Marcus Crassus.

was born the uneasy but tremendously powerful partnership which later came to be known as the First Triumvirate, or three-way ruling coalition.

The Triumvirate's power showed itself almost immediately, for with Pompey's and Crassus's backing, Caesar easily won the consulship. The other elected consul was Marcus Bibulus, who, by coincidence, had also been Caesar's co-aedile four years before. The *optimates* in the Senate had backed Bibulus, counting on his father-in-law, Cato, to control him and ensure that as their lackey he might help to contain Caesar's excesses. But Bibulus, a man of limited talent and fortitude, was no match for Caesar, who rendered his colleague powerless during the first important political fight of the consulship.

This confrontation, which was typical of many that followed, centered around Caesar's submission of a bill that would grant lands to Pompey's veterans and many plebes. The three triumvirs were obviously determined to gain passage of the measures that the Senate had recently denied them. Cato, who led the opposition to the bill, had just begun denouncing it before the Senate when several of Caesar's henchmen suddenly entered, grabbed the flustered senator, and took him into custody. Caesar set Cato free soon afterward, but the episode seemed an ominous sign of the strong-arm tactics that the new consul and his two powerful allies were prepared to utilize.

Indeed, more overt coercion occurred when Caesar brought the same land bill before the Popular Assembly. First, Bibulus spoke against the bill. But then, as Lily Taylor tells it:

> Pompey and Crassus both spoke for the bill, and Pompey made it clear that his troops were at hand to help, if necessary by force, to pass the bill. With Caesar at his side, he [Pompey] was no longer hesitant about the use of force which he had so far never employed in a public assembly. Before the bill came to a vote, Caesar had the Forum occupied by armed men. . . . Bibulus . . . tried [again] to speak against the bill. He was forcibly ejected. . . . Then Cato, who always entered with zest into a fight in the Assembly, tried to force himself to the platform but was also removed after a tumult. The bill was passed in violence and . . . included a clause that all senators were to take an oath to adhere to it.[19]

Afterward, Bibulus was too terrified of Caesar's henchmen to continue with his consular duties. According to Suetonius:

> Caesar's conduct drove him to such a pitch of desperation, that from that time until the end of his term he did not leave his house, but merely issued proclamations announcing adverse omens [signs of doom]. From that time on Caesar managed all the affairs of the state alone and at his own whims; so that various witty fellows, pretending by way of jest to sign and seal official documents, wrote, "Done in the consulship of Julius Caesar," instead of "Bibulus and Caesar."[20]

Like Ruthless Gangsters

Caesar's entire term as consul in the year 59 B.C. was characterized by the same kind of bullying and intimidation. He regularly cut shady deals, ignored or violated legislative rules and laws, and through the threat of force silenced nearly all opposition. All the while, he and his fellow triumvirs grew richer and, like ruthless gangsters, used bribes and fear to spread their influence throughout the government and other social institutions. To help bind the triumvirs, Caesar gave his daughter, Julia, now age seventeen, in marriage to Pompey. At about the same time, Caesar himself married a third time. He had divorced Pompeia in 62, and his new bride was Calpurnia, the daughter of a wealthy former provincial governor named Calpurnius Piso, who openly supported the Triumvirate.

Cicero, Cato, and other conservatives had once worried that the rise of powerful individuals might threaten the state. The advent of the Triumvirate intensified that worry into alarm. Summing up the new political reality, Ernle Bradford comments, "From the moment that these

Caesar with his third wife, Calpurnia, daughter of one of his most important supporters, the wealthy aristocrat Calpurnius Piso.

who was as ambitious as he, decided to change sides and use his might *against* Caesar? Clearly, in order to maintain his power base when no longer a consul, Caesar needed an army loyal to him alone.

One of the few ways to acquire such a military following was to get an appointment as proconsul of an important province. Once in charge of such an area, he could raise whatever troops he needed and then launch a major military campaign, during which his men would become battle-hardened and devoted to him. At the same time, Roman law prohibited the state from prosecuting governors and other high officials for past offenses while they were in office. Therefore, as long as he maintained such a post, the Senate could not arrest him for having broken laws during his tenure as consul.

Two Provinces for the Price of One

With these ideas in mind, in his last months as consul Caesar bypassed the Senate entirely and brought the matter directly to the people. The Popular Assembly wasted no time in giving him two provinces instead of one—Cisalpine Gaul in northernmost Italy and Illyricum directly across the narrow Adriatic Sea from the eastern Italian coast. Moreover, Caesar was to have charge of these territories, each of which came with its own small standing army, for five years instead of the customary one. The *optimates* and his other enemies worried about his acquisition of a private military force but held out the hope that he might lack the talent

three men had decided to pool their resources—military power and fame, monetary power, and political genius—the end of the Republic was in sight."[21]

While the triumvirs continued to ram their own agenda down the government's throat, the always calculating Caesar assessed his present situation and considered how it might affect his future. He had successfully overshadowed the Senate, as he had set out to do. But after his consulship was over, his opponents might try to exact vengeance. For the moment he had Pompey's troops to protect him and to enforce his will, but what if Pompey,

The Desire to Be First

After his praetorship Caesar served in the Roman province of Farther Spain. Both on the journey and while governing there, he often thought about the nature and realities of power, rulers, and military glory. The following two short anecdotes from Plutarch's Life of Caesar *are particularly revealing of Caesar's preoccupation with these concepts:*

"There is a story that while he was crossing the Alps he came to a small village with hardly any inhabitants and altogether a miserable-looking place. His friends were laughing and joking about it, saying: 'No doubt here too one would find people trying hard to gain office, and here too there are struggles to get the first place [in government] and jealous rivalries among the great men.' Caesar then said to them in all seriousness: 'As far as I am concerned, I would rather be the first man here than the second in Rome.'"

"It is also said that . . . when he was in Spain and had some leisure [time], he was reading some part of the history of Alexander [the Great, the Greek general who conquered Egypt and the Persian Empire three centuries before] and, after sitting for a long time lost in his own thoughts, burst into tears. His friends were surprised and asked him the reason. 'Don't you think,' he said, 'that I have something worth being sorry about, when I reflect that at my age Alexander was already king over so many peoples, while I have never yet achieved anything really remarkable?'"

and vision needed to win major battles and army campaigns. "They probably did not realize Caesar's military genius," Lily Taylor points out, because

no one perhaps except Caesar himself suspected that—but they did know that in a long-term command he was getting a chance to build a strong personal army; they also knew that from Cisalpine Gaul he could threaten Italy, and that in a province much of which was inhabited by men with full citizen rights, divided among nearly

half the rural tribes, he would be able to maintain strong pressure on Roman elections.[22]

A Golden Opportunity

But though the senators knew all these things, they unhappily could do nothing about them. The Triumvirate's grip on the government, particularly the Popular Assembly, was strong enough almost to nullify the authority of the Senate, which normally exercised power by exerting influence on the consuls and assembly members. Many senators, including Cicero and Cato, protested by refusing to attend Senate meetings. But this only made Caesar and his cronies even more powerful. For instance, when the aristocrat who had been granted the Narbonese died suddenly, Pompey entered the Senate and demanded that Caesar be awarded this province in addition to the two he already held. The few senators in attendance had neither the means nor the courage to defy Pompey, and they complied with the demand.

Getting his hands on Narbonese Gaul, consisting of the Mediterranean coastal lands of what is now southern France, was an extremely fortunate windfall for Caesar. Beyond the province's northern border stretched hundreds of miles of unknown, untamed territories, rich in nat-ural resources. More importantly, these territories were the home of rustic and warlike tribal societies that had in the past raided Roman lands. Caesar saw clearly that here lay his golden opportunity to lead military conquests as large and important as those of Pompey. According to Suetonius, he was so filled "with joy at this success, he could not keep from boasting a few days later before a crowded house that [he had] gained his heart's desire to the grief . . . of his opponents."[23]

On January 1, 58 B.C., with his consulship officially over, Caesar hurried from Rome and set up a temporary residence in the countryside. According to law, once he was outside the city walls, his proconsulship had begun, and he was immune from prosecution. Caesar now looked northward toward the Alps and the mysterious lands beyond, where he hoped to plant the seeds of a glorious future.

Chapter

3 For the Honor and Glory of Caesar: The Conquest of Gaul

Early in 58 B.C. the forty-two-year-old Caesar left Rome behind and headed north to assume his new duties as proconsul of the Gallic provinces. His real interest, though, was in the more distant reaches of Transalpine Gaul. At the time the Romans had only scanty knowledge of these territories, which stretched northward and westward beyond the boundaries of their own province, the Narbonese. They lacked a clear, realistic idea of the great size of these lands and of the large numbers of people that dwelled in them.

With so few facts to go on, it is likely that Caesar expected the coming campaign to be similar in duration and difficulty to those of other Roman generals. Marius had subdued the Cimbri and Teutones in less than three years, and Pompey had conquered and reorganized vast sections of Asia Minor and the Middle East in less than four. Caesar had no way of knowing that he now faced a challenge far greater than those of his predecessors. Ahead of him lay eight long years of constant danger, large-scale battles and sieges, and seemingly endless and exhausting travel through miles of remote, rugged wilderness.

But no matter how long it took him in Gaul, Caesar intended to accomplish his main and immediate goal. This was to establish himself as a military figure of the same, or even greater, stature as Pompey, while building a strong, loyal personal army. His long-term goal was eventually to return to Rome and resume the exploitation of power he had begun as consul.

This bronze bust of Caesar reveals the same serious, intelligent, and calculating expression depicted in most other surviving sculptures of the famous leader.

"Gaul Consists of Three Separate Parts"

Since Caesar's political enemies, and perhaps his ambitious partners in the Triumvirate, might try to undermine his position in his absence, he could not afford to be out of touch with the capital for too long. Caesar dealt with this problem in two ways. First, he kept a personal journal describing his military adventures in great detail. He sent regular installments of this journal, which became known as the *Commentaries on the Gallic War*, back to Rome so that both the Senate and the public would have a constant reminder of his exploits and his enduring power. Second, with the help of two able assistants, Cornelius Balbus and Gaius Oppius, Caesar maintained a network of agents and messengers. Lily Taylor explains that in Rome at the time:

> There was no police force, no postal or freight service, and, except in the treasury, practically no civil service. The nobles looked after their personal safety by keeping up bands of followers and attendants. They communicated with the cities of Italy and the provinces through personal messengers, using vehicles [chariots or wagons], horses, or ships which were their private property. . . . Caesar's organization of his contacts in Rome through the loyal Balbus was remarkably efficient during his years of absence in Gaul. There was a steady stream of messengers between Rome and Gaul, and Caesar was informed of everything [that happened in Italy shortly after it occurred]. Balbus, later aided

by the equally efficient Oppius, did wonders in upholding Caesar's influence and seeing to it that the men [in Rome] whom Caesar supported lived up to their obligations.[24]

Satisfied that he could retain his power base in Rome while away in the provinces, Caesar assessed the present situation in Gaul and considered his first move. Most of what little the Romans knew about Transalpine Gaul beyond the Narbonese came from reports by Gallic nomads and merchants who traded with Roman border communities. These traders described in general terms the peoples who inhabited the lands bordered in the west by the Atlantic Ocean and in the east by the Rhine River. The Rhine was recognized by Romans and Gauls alike as the boundary between Gaul and the Germanic territories, the home of several fierce and rugged tribal peoples.

Probably no one at the time, inside or outside of Gaul, realized that Gaul itself contained over two hundred distinct tribes. Many of these tribes shared common roots and had similar customs and languages. So it became customary to lump them together into a few broad groups. Caesar himself did so in the famous opening lines of his *Commentaries*:

> The country of Gaul consists of three separate parts, one of which [in the far north] is inhabited by the Belgae, one [in the southwest] by the Aquitani, and one [in the central region] by the people whom we call "Gauls" but who are known in their own language as "Celts." These three peoples differ from one another in language, customs and laws. . . . The toughest soldiers come from the Belgae. This is

Tough, bearded horsemen like these were among the nomadic Gauls whom Caesar and his legions opposed and eventually conquered in the 50s B.C.

because they are farthest away from the culture and civilized way of life of the Roman Province [the Narbonese] . . . and they are also nearest to the Germans across the Rhine and are continually waging war with them. For the same reason the Helvetii are the bravest tribe among the Gauls; they too are in almost daily contact with the Germans, either fighting to keep them out of Gaul or launching attacks on them in their own territory.[25]

Uncivilized Barbarians?

Fortunately for Caesar, who craved an excuse to launch a military campaign, potential trouble was brewing in central Gaul at about the same time that he assumed his proconsulship. The Helvetii, harassed by their Germanic eastern neighbors, were preparing to leave their homeland in what is now northern Switzerland. Caesar had heard reports that the Helvetii, numbering over three hundred thousand, had decided, in his words, "to prepare all the necessary arrangements for a mass migration. They were to buy up all the wagons and pack animals that they could, sow as much grain as possible so as to have adequate supplies on the march, and make treaties of friendship with neighboring states."[26]

Caesar and other Roman leaders feared that this mass migration would overrun the northern part of the Narbonese. It might also set in motion a series of tribal wars that would further threaten Roman lands. Caesar saw as his first great task, therefore, to contain the Helvetii. Like most Romans, he arrogantly viewed them and the other non-Roman inhabitants of Gaul as uncivilized barbarians, inferiors whose lives and futures Rome had a right and a duty to control.

What Caesar did not realize at the time was that the Gauls were far from uncivilized. As historian Donald R. Dudley comments:

The free society of Celtic Gaul which Caesar was about to demolish was the most advanced culture which had yet appeared north of the Alps. It was commonly underestimated by classical [Greek and Roman] writers, since it lacked some of the features which they regarded as essential for civilization. It had no cities, for example . . . although centers of population had begun to grow up round the dwellings of powerful nobles, or for purposes of trade and industry. . . . Socially, the Celtic world was dominated by great nobles living on their country estates with their kinsmen and vassals [dependent workers]. They had long valued the luxury products of the classical world, especially its wine and metalware. But the Celts were themselves skilled workers in metals—iron, bronze, and gold. . . . Moreover, the Celts were skilled agriculturalists . . . feeding the very large population of Gaul on the produce of the land. They were especially skilled with horses, their breeding, and their use in war and for transport.[27]

Caesar Versus the Helvetii

Without regard for the Helvetii's civilized skills or for their persecution by the Germans, who had driven them to the migration they were planning, Caesar marched his army northward, intent on armed confrontation. He had three legions, military divisions of about five to six thousand soldiers each, which he had collected in Cisalpine Gaul. When he reached the Narbonese, he was reinforced by its single standing legion, giving him a total force of perhaps twenty-four thousand troops. Almost immediately, this number began steadily increasing as his agents recruited more soldiers from both Cisalpine and Narbonese Gaul.

In April of 58 B.C., Caesar approached the Helvetii near the Saone River, not far north of the Narbonese. The Helvetii chiefs sent a delegation informing the Roman leader that their people had no intention of entering the nearby Roman province. They did not want to fight and only desired to travel westward until they could find suitable unoccupied lands to settle. Ignoring this peaceful overture, Caesar attacked the already migrating tribe as it attempted to cross the river. Although the Helvetii had perhaps as many as ninety thousand armed warriors, at that moment most of them were mixed in among their women and children in a massive train of people, animals, and wagons

This drawing depicts the Helvetii leaders planning their mass migration through Gaul. They told Caesar that their intentions were peaceable and that they wanted only to pass through Roman lands briefly on their way west.

This depiction of the Helvetii's migration, produced many centuries after the real event, inaccurately shows the tribesmen clad in European garb of a later period.

that stretched over many miles. As a result, the Romans encountered minimal organized resistance and massacred the "enemy" by the thousands.

The bulk of the Helvetii escaped and continued westward. But a few weeks later Caesar caught up with them. Near Armecy, in south-central Gaul, he engaged them in what proved to be the first important battle of his career. "Hurling their spears from above," Caesar recorded,

> our men easily broke up the enemy's mass formation and, having achieved this, drew their swords and charged. In the fighting the Gauls were seriously hampered because several of their overlapping shields were often pierced by a single spear; the iron head would bend and they could neither get it out nor fight properly with their left arms. . . . In the end the

wounds and the toil of battle were too much for them and . . . when they could stand up to us no longer . . . the enemy retreated. . . . In the whole of this battle, which had lasted from midday until the evening, not a single [Roman] man was seen to turn and run. Around the [enemy camp's] stockade, fighting went on far into the night.[28]

Caesar's victory halted the Helvetii's westward migration and the survivors eventually returned to their original farms and villages in the northern Alpine foothills. According to Caesar's reckoning, his men had killed 258,000 members of the tribe. This fantastic figure was undoubtedly an exaggeration intended to impress his readers in Rome. The actual number of casualties was much lower—perhaps sixty to eighty thousand—although this still represented a horrific and tragic slaughter.

A Fierce and Courageous People

After the Helvetii's downfall, many of the tribes of central Gaul, fearing that the Romans might target them next, sent envoys to Caesar asking for peace treaties. The Aedui, now the dominant tribe in the region, even offered to become Roman allies. The Aedui chiefs and some other Gallic leaders then asked Caesar to deal with the Germans, who had stepped up their raids into eastern Gaul. He immediately agreed, since he had already been contemplating just such an action. These bold Germanic tribesmen were related to the Cimbri and Teutones who had posed a

Nothing Less than a Masterpiece

Caesar's military journal, the Commentaries, *has been translated, read, and studied extensively by both scholars and schoolchildren through the ages. The following description and insightful critique of the work is by the prolific historian Michael Grant in his excellent biography, titled simply* Caesar.

"The *Gallic War* and subsequent *Civil War* were entitled *Commentaries,* a term which, with unwarranted modesty, deliberately falls somewhat short of 'Histories,' denoting rather a set of commander's dispatches or memoranda, amplified partly by speeches (intended as always in antiquity [ancient times], to give background rather than represent exact words). . . . Caesar's enormous brain power and exceedingly lucid [clear], compact, Latin style transform this apparently unambitious work into nothing less than a major masterpiece. The fact that the Roman commander-in-chief was its author (except for the last of its eight books, which was written by one of his generals, Aulus Hirtius) brings great advantages and disadvantages alike. The advantages lie in the extraordinary authority conferred by the author's unique inside knowledge, and by all the manifold [diverse] talents which he could bring to bear upon its presentation to the reader. The disadvantages reside in Caesar's personal preoccupations [interests and biases], and most of all his desire to refute his political enemies in Rome. This sometimes induced him to magnify, minimize, and distort—though it is usually the implications [the way he interprets or judges the importance of the facts] rather than the facts [themselves] that suffer, since Caesar . . . was far too good a hand at publicity to lie more than was absolutely necessary."

Ariovistus (left, on horseback) unwisely brags of his power and courage to Caesar (the other horseman) shortly before the battle in which the Romans annihilated most of the Germanic war leader's tribe.

threat to southern Gaul a generation before. Now united under a war chief named Ariovistus, their army was camped on the western side of the Rhine.

In the autumn of 58 B.C., Caesar led six legions against Ariovistus. In a savage battle, the legions sent the Germans into a desperate retreat. While the enemy fled, the Romans overran their camp and killed most of their women and children. Caesar's overwhelming victory and subsequent act of shocking cruelty sent a wave of fear through other nearby German tribes. "When news of the battle reached the other side of the Rhine," he wrote, "the Suebi, who had advanced as far as the banks of the river, began to go home again."[29] Afterward, the Rhine frontier remained quiet for several years.

After wintering in Cisalpine Gaul, Caesar next turned his attention to the fierce Belgae in the northern reaches of Transalpine Gaul. In the summer of 57, he marched eight legions, forty-five to fifty thousand troops, to the Aisne River in what is now northeastern France. If the Belgic tribes had managed to unite, they could have fielded perhaps three hundred thousand warriors, a force even Caesar would have been hard pressed to deal with. However, they remained disunited, giving him the advantage of fighting them one at a time.

One of the Belgic tribes did give the Romans the fight of their lives. These were the Nervii, described by Caesar as "a fierce people and extremely courageous," who "declared that they would never send envoys to us and never accept any kind of peace."[30] As Plutarch told it, in a thickly wooded section of what is now Belgium, the Nervii warriors

suddenly fell upon Caesar with a force of 60,000 men at a time when he was fortifying a camp and had no idea that the battle was impending. They routed Caesar's cavalry, surrounded the seventh and twelfth legions, and killed all their centurions [unit leaders]. In all probability the Romans would have been destroyed to the last man if Caesar himself had not snatched up a

The Tools of a Soldier's Trade

The extreme efficiency and devastating power of Caesar's legions were due partly to the soldiers' expert use of very lethal, and at the same time flexible, weapons and armor. In his detailed biography of Caesar, historian Ernle Bradford offers this overview of what he calls a first-century B.C. Roman legionnaire's "tools of the trade":

"By the time of Caesar the arms of the legionnaire had been streamlined . . . into two only—the sword and spear. Swords were basically of a type that the Romans had first encountered in Spain. They had a double cutting edge and a stabbing-point, were sheathed in a metal-bound leather scabbard, and hung on the legionnaire's right hand side. . . . The spears came in two main types; both were throwing spears known as a *pilum*, and one was light-weight and the other a heavy-weight. . . . The Caesarian legionnaire was protected by a mail shirt [made of thin, jointed metal scales] that hung about half way down his thighs, under which he wore a leather jerkin, and on his head what is called a Montefortino helmet (so-called after the cemetery where an example was found). This type of helmet had protective cheek pieces and was pear-shaped, rising to a lead-filled top-knot which held a horsehair crest. A rim ran around the bottom of the helmet, swept out farther at the back to protect the neck against glancing blows. The shield was oval-shaped and . . . was made from laminated [coated] strips of wood. . . . Shields were often leather covered. . . . Greaves [lower-leg protectors] were rarely worn by the ordinary legionnaire, and his equipment ended in his heavy leather sandals . . . laced over the foot and up around the ankles, the soles studded with iron nails."

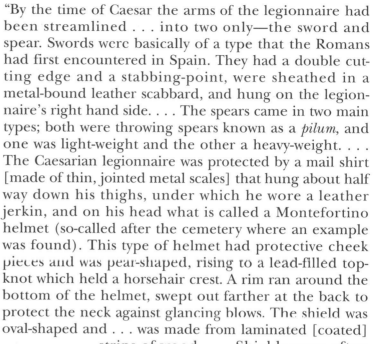

The Roman soldier at left wears a lorca squamata, *a tunic of armor scales, and holds a* cornu, *a curved battle trumpet; the other man wears a* lorca segmentata, *a leather tunic with attached metal strips.*

shield, forced his way through to the front of the fighting, and hurled himself on the natives. . . . Caesar's personal daring had its effect; in the fighting his men went, as the saying is, beyond themselves—though even then they never made the Nervii turn and run, but cut them down fighting on to the end. Out of 60,000 only 500 are said to have survived the battle, and out of their governing body of 400 only three remained alive.[31]

Caesar's Camp Was Their Fatherland

Caesar's stirring personal display against the Nervii was but one example of the raw courage, fighting skill, and physical prowess that he showed throughout the Gallic wars. Suetonius wrote:

> He was highly skilled in arms and horsemanship, and of incredible powers of endurance. On the march he headed his army, sometimes on horseback, but oftener on foot, bareheaded both in the heat of the sun and in the rain. He covered great distances with incredible speed . . . very often arriving before the messengers sent to announce his coming.[32]

Such impressive physical feats naturally earned him the respect of his men, who had never before encountered such a larger-than-life figure.

All through the Gallic campaigns, Caesar used other means of raising his men's morale and grooming them into an awesome professional fighting force com-

Caesar addresses his troops. His close bond with them contributed greatly to his success as a general.

pletely devoted to him. He overhauled training methods, improved weapons quality, and made camp life more ordered and efficient. He also doubled the soldiers' regular pay and frequently granted them bonuses, a revolutionary policy at the time. In addition, he took a keen and apparently sincere interest in his men's personal needs and problems, often touring his camp and engaging in long and spirited one-on-one conversations. It is no wonder, then, that, as Plutarch remarked:

> His ability to secure the affection of his men and to get the best out of them was remarkable. Soldiers who in other campaigns had not shown themselves to be any better than the average became irresistible and invincible and ready to confront any danger,

once it was a question of fighting for Caesar's honor and glory.[33]

Famed historian Michael Grant summed it up well in his book *The Army of the Caesars*: "Their fatherland was Caesar's camp, and their patriotism was loyalty to Caesar."[34]

As Caesar had expected, his powerful personal military force proved essential to his maintaining a state of equality with the other two triumvirs. While he was away in Gaul, the Triumvirate began to deteriorate. Pompey grew increasingly jealous as people daily compared Caesar's exploits to his own, and Crassus longed to lead his own glorious expedition. Meanwhile, Cicero shrewdly attempted to play the triumvirs against one another in hopes of reasserting senatorial authority. It finally became clear to Caesar and his partners that they needed a face-to-face meeting to patch up the cracks in their alliance.

This meeting occurred in April 56 B.C. in Luca, in the southern part of Cisalpine Gaul. The three men managed to hammer

---

A Useful Building Style

While in Gaul, Caesar's interests ranged over more than just military operations and battles. He keenly observed the plants, animals, and climate of the country, as well as the religion, customs, lifestyles, and building methods of the native peoples. He recorded several of these observations in his Commentaries, *giving in Book Seven this description of local defensive walls:*

"Nearly all Gallic town walls are built on the following plan. Beams of timber are laid on the ground at intervals of two feet all along the length of the wall and at right angles to it. The beams are then fastened together on the inside and banked up with a good lot of earth; the intervals between them are fitted in with large stones facing outward. When this course has been laid and the beams tightly fastened together, another course is laid on top of it. This is arranged so that, while the same interval is maintained between the beams, those of the second course are not in contact with those of the first, but are laid on a layer of stones two feet high. Thus each beam has one stone between it and the one below and is kept firmly in position. Course is added to course in the same way until the wall reaches the required height. This is an agreeable style of building to look at. It is also, from a practical point of view, a style that is very useful for the defense of cities. The stone gives protection from fire and the wood resists battering rams, which can neither breach nor shake to bits a structure that is secured on the inside by beams which generally run to a length of forty feet."

---

out an agreement that satisfied the immediate ambitions of each. Pompey and Crassus would become the consuls for the following year, Pompey would receive a five-year proconsulship over both Spanish provinces, and Crassus would command an expedition against Parthia. Located in the Middle East beyond Asia Minor, Parthia had not provoked a Roman invasion. But it was one of the few rich unconquered lands left on Rome's borders, and Crassus saw it as a tempting prize to exploit. Caesar walked away from the meeting with a five-year extension of his Gallic and Illyric proconsulships. In addition, he transferred Cicero's brother, an army officer named Quintus, to his command in Gaul, a move designed to intimidate the famous senator. Cicero did remain quiet for a time, although whether this was due to concern for his brother's safety or to the continuing impotence of the Senate is unknown.

To the Beaches of Britain

Immediately after the meeting at Luca, Caesar began drawing long-range plans for further conquests. With Transalpine Gaul seemingly pacified, he was determined to switch his base of operations to Illyricum and begin raids northward into the German-held lands of central Europe. He proposed at some later date also to launch an expedition to the distant and largely mysterious island of Britain. Fabled as having large supplies of gold, tin, and pearls, Britain lay a few miles off the coast of northwestern Gaul, a region later called Brittany.

It was in Brittany that a sudden crisis occurred later in 56 B.C. that upset Caesar's plans. The Veneti, a maritime tribe with a powerful fleet of warships, seized some of Caesar's officers who had been visiting the area and threatened to make war on the Romans. This gave Caesar two causes for worry. First, the Veneti might incite other pacified Gallic tribes to revolt, and second, he needed to use Brittany as a base of operations for his invasion of Britain. Wasting no time, he sent orders for a Roman fleet to move up Gaul's western coast. He himself raced overland, and in the waters near Brittany he and his capable officer, Decimus Albinus, delivered the Veneti a crushing defeat.

Since he was now camped in Brittany with both ships and legions, Caesar decided that there was no point in putting off his proposed expedition to Britain. After making preparations, in July 55 he crossed the waterway that would later be known as the English Channel, taking with him two legions in about eighty ships. The landing in southern Britain was difficult because the native Britons, people of Celtic origin like many Gauls, knew the Romans were coming. Describing how the Britons attacked his men as they tried to disembark, Caesar wrote:

> Both sides fought fiercely. Among our men, however, there was considerable disorder, since it was impossible for them to keep ranks, stand firmly in position, or follow proper standards. . . . The enemy knew all the shallows; and when they saw from the beach any party of our men disembarking one by one from a ship, they spurred their horses into the water and attacked while we were at a dis-

Caesar's troops fight their way ashore in their famous landing on the beaches of Britain.

advantage and they could swarm around a few of us at a time in superior numbers.[35]

The Romans eventually managed to push back the attackers and establish a beachhead. But soon afterward, a sudden storm wrecked many of Caesar's ships, and unusually high tides damaged others. He felt it prudent to return to Gaul and come back to Britain later with a much larger invasion force. He led this second expedition, consisting of five legions and two thousand cavalry riding some eight hundred ships, across the channel in June of the following year. This time Caesar was a bit more successful, managing to capture the Britons' southern capital at what is now St. Albans, north of London. However, storms again damaged large numbers of his ships, and it became increasingly difficult to keep his men supplied. Even more serious, reports came in daily from Gaul reporting increasing native unrest and uprisings. In the autumn of 54 Caesar abandoned Britain a second time and returned to Gaul. His mood must have been somber at that moment for two reasons. First, the British adventure had been the only military campaign in his career that was not an overwhelming success. Second, the sad news reached him that his daughter, Julia, had died in childbirth and that the baby, Pompey's son, had died with her.

A Stunning Triumph

But Caesar found little time to grieve. The Belgae suddenly rebelled and attacked a Roman camp, massacring more than seven thousand legionnaires. As Belgic warriors moved against another Roman contingent, its commander, Quintus Cicero, heroically held off the enemy hordes until Caesar arrived with reinforcements. Ironically, the man Caesar had transferred for political reasons had turned out to be a valuable military asset. The Romans were eventually able to contain the Belgae, but a few months later, in 52 B.C., the central region of Gaul exploded. Many tribes joined this great insurrection, which was spearheaded by the formidable Arverni tribe, led by the war chief Vercingetorix, the most capable military leader Gaul ever produced.

At first, Vercingetorix wisely retreated before Caesar, destroying local crops and livestock so that the Romans could not use them. The Arverni finally attacked Caesar's forces, but the Romans beat them back, and Vercingetorix retired with his army to his fortress at Alesia, in north-central Gaul. Caesar surrounded and laid siege to Alesia. While the siege was in progress, however, a huge army made up of contingents from many neighboring tribes arrived and surrounded the Romans. For four tumultuous days, Caesar, his forces badly outnumbered, led a brilliant and effective defense against almost relentless attacks from all sides. Describing his climactic charge and subsequent victory, he recorded in his journal:

> The enemy could see that I was coming because of the scarlet cloak which I always wore to mark me out in action. And as the lower slopes along which I came were visible from the higher ground, they could also see the squadrons of cavalry and the cohorts [troop units] which I had ordered to follow me. So the enemy rushed into battle. The shout [war cry] was raised on both sides. . . . Our men dispensed with spears and got to work with their swords. Suddenly the Gauls saw our cavalry coming in from the rear; fresh cohorts of infantry were also bearing down. The enemy turned and ran. As they ran, the cavalry were upon them. There was a great slaughter.[36]

After Caesar's stunning triumph, Vercingetorix surrendered, and the great Gallic rebellion collapsed. By the end of 51 B.C., the Romans were in firm control of nearly all of Transalpine Gaul. During almost eight years in Gaul and Britain, Caesar had fought more than thirty major battles, captured more than eight hundred towns, and killed over a million people, an impressive or despicable record, depending on one's point of view.

The Triumvirate in Shambles

Most of the common people in Italy, including the capital, were certainly impressed by Caesar's conquests, and he longed to march into his native city at the head of great triumph. However, the situation among the ruling elite in Rome was now much different from when he had left for the provinces. Crassus had met disastrous defeat and death in Parthia in 53 B.C., and in the following two years Caesar's enemies had managed to turn Pompey against Caesar.

With the Triumvirate in shambles and Pompey's army in control of Rome, Caesar now faced the most crucial decision of his life. A proconsul was expected to give up command of his army at the conclusion of his term of office. Caesar realized that if he did this, he would lose the instrument of power he had worked so long to create. Yet his return to Rome at the head of his army would be considered an act of armed rebellion against the state, which Pompey would then surely defend with his own troops. Caesar took his time making this decision. He knew that whichever path he chose would profoundly affect his future, as well as that of his country and the entire Mediterranean world.

Chapter

4 "The Die Is Cast": Civil War Engulfs the Roman World

It had not been Caesar's original intention to involve himself and his country in a bloody civil war. All through his Gallic campaigns, he planned on returning to Rome in triumph, regaining the office of consul, and resuming his high position in Roman power politics. The one problem that might upset these plans was the possibility of government prosecution. If, when his proconsulship was up, he returned to Rome for the July 49 B.C. elections, the Senate might arrest him for past offenses before he could assume the consulship on January 1, 48. In order to prevent such an occurrence, while still governor Caesar mobilized his considerable political forces in the capital. He had his supporters push through a special law allowing him to run for the consulship *in absentia*, or in his absence. That way, he could be a candidate while still in his own province and then, after winning, enter Rome early in 48 without fear of arrest.

But by the end of the year 50, many senators and other officials had made it clear that they would not honor the *in absentia* law. Using trusted assistants, including Marcus Antonius, or Mark Antony, Caesar tried to sway the opposition by offering various political deals. The *optimates* in the capital offered counterdeals. And in the meantime they continued to woo

Pompey. As Caesar himself put it, Pompey

> had been pushed into action by my enemies, and also by his own wish that no one should be placed on the same level as himself. He had entirely broken off his old friendship with me and had become friends again with those who had been enemies of us both,

According to ancient sources, Mark Antony, who began his career as Caesar's assistant, was a skilled and daring soldier, but a vain and crude man.

most of whom he personally had turned against me during the time that he was my son-in-law.[37]

The crisis came to a head in December 50, when the Senate called for Caesar to lay down command of his army. At the same time, the government extended Pompey's Spanish proconsulship by several years in order to allow him to keep command of his own army. Despite Antony's energetic efforts in Caesar's behalf, on January 7, 49, the government boldly relieved Caesar of his proconsulship. "Decrees of the most savage and insulting kind were passed depriving me of my command," Caesar later wrote.[38] That same day, faced with numerous threats for their personal safety, Antony and his close colleagues fled the city and joined Caesar, who was camped on the far side of the Rubicon River. Caesar realized that if, at the head of his army, he crossed this recognized border between Cisalpine Gaul and Italy proper, he would plunge Rome into a state of civil war. But at that moment he could see no other course. "He paused for a while," wrote Suetonius,

and realizing what a step he was taking, he turned to those about him and said, "Even yet we may turn back; but once we cross that little bridge . . . the whole issue is with the sword." Then Caesar cried, "Take we the course which the signs of the gods and the false dealing of our foes point out. The die is cast," he said.[39]

Caesar leads his men across the Rubicon River. This fateful act ignited a destructive civil war that dragged on for five years.

With these words, on January 10, 49 B.C., Caesar crossed the Rubicon. Thus began a devastating conflict that would engulf the whole Mediterranean world and eventually vault Caesar to the position he so cherished—that of ultimate power.

Caesar's Enemies in Flight

Clearly, Caesar's opponents had not expected him to make such a bold move. Certainly they did not dream that the Italian towns between Cisalpine Gaul and Rome would, one by one, eagerly open their gates and welcome Caesar in his fateful southward march. And yet they did. The result was fear and chaos in Rome. While various factions—Pompey, the consuls, and the Senate—vied for authority, no one wanted to face Caesar and his battle-hardened legions. Most fled southward, and Caesar encountered no resistance when he entered Rome. When it became clear that for the time being he could not mount a credible defense against Caesar, Pompey hurried to the port of Brundisium, on the eastern tip of the Italian boot. There he and many of Caesar's other enemies prepared to escape to Greece.

Caesar soon traveled to Brundisium and attempted a last-ditch reconciliation with Pompey. "I still thought that no opportunity for making peace should be neglected," Caesar recorded in his journal. "What I wanted most of all was to have an interview with Pompey. If this chance were given me . . . I was very confident indeed that fair terms could be found for a cessation of hostilities on both sides."[40] But for reasons that remain unclear, Pompey passed up this chance to avoid all-out war and sailed for Greece.

Now holding virtually complete authority over Italy, Caesar decided it would be prudent to make this authority appear as legitimate as possible. This would require the Senate's stamp of approval. Seeking senatorial support, he approached Cicero, the leading figure among the few senators who had opted to stay and face him. Cicero informed his longtime opponent that his conscience dictated he support Pompey and the consuls instead. Directly after this meeting, Cicero wrote to a friend:

> He [Caesar] said my decision amounted to condemning him, and that if I did not [support him in the Senate] others would be reluctant to do so. . . . The upshot was that, by way of ending the interview, he asked me to think it over. To this I could not say no, and so we parted. The result is that I don't think he is very pleased with me.[41]

Indeed, Caesar was quite displeased with Cicero and other senators who refused him support and advice. When it became clear that he would not get any sort of official blessing for his cause, Caesar declared that he would run the country himself in any way he saw fit. To emphasize this point, he marched to the national treasury, housed in the Temple of Saturn, and transferred the state's money to his own coffers. For all intents and purposes, from this time on, republican government in Rome ceased to exist. Cicero, last great defender of the republic, was heartbroken over the terrible civil strife he saw on the horizon. "So vast are the forces which I see

"War Has No Use for Free Speech"

Before leaving to confront Pompey's forces in Spain, Caesar went to the national treasury, planning to take money to finance his campaigns. As Plutarch described it in his Life of Caesar, *the general had first to contend with a stalwart public official, the tribune Metellus, who daringly tried to stop him:*

"When Metellus, the tribune, tried to prevent Caesar from taking money from the state reserve and began to cite various laws, Caesar told him that there was a time for laws and a time for arms. 'As for you,' he said, 'if you don't like what is being done, get out of the way for the present. War has no use for free speech. But when I have laid down my arms and come to terms, then you can come back again and make your speeches to the people. And let me point out that in saying this I am giving up my own just rights. In fact you are my prisoner.' . . . After saying this to Metellus, Caesar went toward the doors of the treasury and, as the keys could not be found, sent for [black]smiths and ordered them to break the doors down. Metellus once again began to object and there were some [onlookers] who applauded him for doing so. Caesar then raised his voice and threatened to kill him if he did not stop interfering. 'And, young man,' he said, 'you know well enough that I dislike saying this more than I would dislike doing it.' These words had their effect. Metellus went off in a fright and for the future all Caesar's demands for material for the war were promptly and readily obeyed."

Caesar opens the doors of the Roman treasury after confronting a tribune named Metellus, who had bravely but only temporarily blocked his way.

will take part in the conflict on both sides," he wrote. "Nothing can exceed the misery, ruin and disgrace. . . . The sun seems to me to have disappeared from the universe."[42] Sadly, Cicero gathered his belongings, left his beloved Rome, and joined Pompey in Greece.

Caesar as Dictator

At the time, Pompey was consolidating his forces for the fight against Caesar. In many ways, Pompey's position was the stronger of the two. His prior conquests had been in the eastern Mediterranean, and he still maintained a strong power base in the conquered Greek kingdoms. Moreover, he still controlled most of Rome's fleets, giving him overall command of the sea. And his armies in the Spanish provinces, over which he remained proconsul, were still steadfastly loyal to him.

Thus Caesar faced the daunting task of fighting a war on both eastern and western fronts. In order to keep Pompey's forces from enveloping him on both sides, Caesar decided to eliminate the western front as quickly as possible. Initiating a lightning campaign, Caesar hurried an army of thirty-five thousand men toward Spain. On the way, he stopped in what is now southern France and began a siege of Massilia (later Marseille), a prosperous and strategically located Greek city that had openly shown its support for Pompey. Leaving some trusted officers to continue the siege, Caesar moved on and arrived in Spain in June 49 B.C.

There, for several weeks he played a cat-and-mouse game with Pompey's two able commanders, Lucius Afranius and Marcus Petreius, who were reluctant to engage in a battle with Caesar's more numerous and experienced soldiers. Eventually Caesar managed to cut off his opponents' supplies of grain and water. Faced with a choice between starvation or annihilation, Afranius and Petreius surrendered at Ilerda, in northern Spain, on August 27. Caesar's enemies in Greece were stunned when they learned that he had taken control of Spain in a mere two months without even fighting a battle.

Wasting no time, Caesar departed Spain, passed back through Massilia, which had recently fallen to his forces, and returned to Rome. He still wanted to be elected consul, but that was now impossible. According to Roman law, the consular election had to be run by the serving consuls and they were presently helping Pompey rally his forces in Greece. So Caesar had his own supporters in the Assembly immediately push through a resolution declaring him dictator, a position he claimed he was assuming in order to "save" the state from Pompey.

Restoring Public Confidence

At this juncture, Caesar showed that, although he clearly desired to wield supreme power, he had both the capacity and the will to use that power in constructive ways. Only hours after becoming dictator, he tackled a problem that threatened to destroy Rome's economy. With the deteriorating political situation and looming civil war, many rich people hoarded their money or took it out of Italy. Because money was in short supply and times were hard, hundreds of thousands of Romans could not pay their debts, and land and other valuables became increasingly worthless. To save the economy, Caesar forbade the hoarding of money and also declared that prices were to revert to the level where they were *before* the beginning of the civil war. "I found," the dictator recorded in his *Commentaries,*

> that throughout Italy credit was becoming restricted and debts were not being paid, and so I decided to appoint assessors to make a valuation of real and personal property on a prewar basis, so that creditors should be paid accordingly. This seemed to be the most appropriate means for removing or diminishing the fear of a general cancellation of debts [which would ruin creditors and collapse the economy]—a fear which is very often felt in periods of war and civil disturbances—and also for maintaining credit.[43]

Caesar's bold financial initiatives quickly restored public confidence in lending and spending money, and the economy steadily improved.

On the Plain of Pharsalus

Caesar's assumption of the dictatorship and able handling of the money crisis took him only eleven days, after which he directed all of his attention to the campaign against Pompey. Traditionally, for fear of losing ships and men in bad weather, the Romans refrained from large-scale naval operations during the winter. So Pompey and his commanders did not

A later European drawing of a triumphant Caesar in ceremonial garb and wearing a crown of laurel leaves.

expect Caesar to cross over to Greece until the spring. But Caesar was not about to let tradition interfere with his usual speed and decisiveness. In January 48 B.C. he gathered what few ships he could and ferried part of his forces—about twenty thousand infantry and six hundred cavalry—across the Adriatic to northwestern Greece. Using largely the same ships, Antony soon followed with another twenty thousand to twenty-four thousand infantry and eight hundred cavalry.

Though Caesar had appeared in Greece sooner than anyone had expected,

Pompey, having amassed an army nearly twice as large as his opponent's, was more than adequately prepared. Most of Pompey's new recruits, like many of Caesar's own men, were neither of Italian birth nor Roman citizens. In fact, as Michael Grant points out, Pompey had

organized the most ambitious mobilization of non-citizens that had ever been known. This was an occasion when for the first time whole legions began to be formed of non-Italians. . . . Both commanders . . . had now wholly abandoned the traditional republican reluctance to arm provincials [natives of Rome's provinces]. Spaniards had already been extensively enrolled by both sides and now

Enemy Treachery

During Caesar's siege of the Greek city of Massilia in 49 B.C., at one point the defenders attempted an elaborate ruse to trick Caesar's men into dropping their guard. In this excerpt from his Commentaries on the Civil War, *Caesar described how his men were surprised to see the townspeople rush*

"out of one of the gates in a body [together], unarmed, with fillets [ribbons] round their heads, and, with their hands outstretched like suppliants [worshipers], appealing for mercy to the officers and men of our forces. This strange sight brought military operations to a standstill. . . . The enemy, on reaching our lines, all fell down together at the feet of our army and its commanders. They begged them not to take any further action till I had arrived; their city, they said, was obviously practically in our hands now that our siege works [machines and battlements] were finished. . . . Simply out of compassion a sort of truce was arranged to operate until I should arrive. Not a shot was fired either from the walls or from our lines and, as it was assumed that everything was over, people generally relaxed and took things easily. . . . The enemy, however, were without any sense of honor. They were merely waiting for a suitable opportunity to show treachery and deceit. They let a few days pass and then suddenly burst out of their gates at midday when our men were tired out or at their ease. . . . The enemy set fire to the siege works. . . . This sudden disaster roused our men to action. . . . An attack was made on the enemy, who took to flight. . . . So the labor of several months was destroyed in a mere moment by enemy treachery."

The Centurion Keeps His Promise

In this well-known excerpt from his Life of Pompey, *Plutarch described the courage of one of Caesar's centurions, or unit commanders, who was the first or one of the first to make contact with the enemy at the battle of Pharsalus:*

"On both sides the signal for battle was raised; and from Caesar's army the first man to charge forwards out of the ranks was Gaius Crassianus, a centurion in command of 120 men. He had promised Caesar much and he was keeping his promise. For Crassianus had been the first man whom Caesar saw as he came out of the camp that day, and Caesar had asked him how he felt about the battle. Then Crassianus . . . shouted out: 'You are going to win, Caesar, and win gloriously. And as for me, you shall praise me today, whether I am alive or dead at the end of it.' Now Crassianus kept these words of his in mind. He rushed forward, with many others following his example, and plunged into the middle of the enemy ranks. Close fighting with swords began immediately and many were killed; and so the centurion forced his way forward, cutting down the men in the front ranks until one of them stood up to him and drove in at his mouth with such force that the point came through at the back of his neck."

Pompey mobilized peoples such as the Dardani and Bessi [from the remote lands northeast of Illyricum]. . . . As for Caesar, he [had] cavalry from Gaul and Germany, and archers and slingers from the Balearic Islands [off the Spanish coast]. Roman armies were becoming much more cosmopolitan [made up of diverse elements]. And these soldiers of many races felt little interest in the Roman state, which had now become a rather vague and abstract conception. All that mattered was their own commander, with whom they were [closely] linked by bonds of mutual [need].[44]

In early August 48, Caesar camped on the edge of a plain near the small town of Pharsalus in east-central Greece. After a few days, Pompey's larger army arrived and on the morning of August 9 the commanders lined up their forces between the town and a wide stream. Pompey realized that his seven thousand horsemen greatly outnumbered Caesar's cavalry unit of no more than fourteen hundred. To take advantage of this numerical superiority, Pompey placed the right end, or wing, of his army, a contingent composed of infantry, against the stream. The water, he reasoned, would act as a barrier to keep Caesar's troops from outflanking, or moving around and in back of, his own. Pompey then put all of his cavalry on his left wing, directly opposite the cavalry that made up Caesar's right wing. Pompey planned for his horsemen to smash Caesar's cavalry and then proceed to outflank Caesar's infantry. In his journal, Caesar later explained his opponent's plan, quoting Pompey as telling his own officers:

> I have discussed this plan with our cavalry commanders and they have undertaken to carry it out. What they will do is this. When the two armies draw close together, they will attack Caesar's right wing on its open flank, ride around, and encircle his line from the rear, thus throwing his army into confusion and routing [defeating] the whole force before our troops have even thrown their spears. In this way we shall finish the war without exposing our legions to any risk and probably without any casualties at all.[45]

It is difficult to believe that an experienced general like Pompey could expect to defeat an opponent of Caesar's caliber without any casualties. Pompey was undoubtedly painting an overly rosy picture in order to instill confidence in his men, although he apparently did believe his planned maneuver would defeat Caesar. In this, Pompey was guilty of gross overconfidence. Seeing how his opponent was placing his cavalry, Caesar immediately devised a countermeasure. Blocked from Pompey's view by Caesar's horsemen, three thousand of Caesar's best fighters stealthily moved behind these horsemen into a position from which to spring a deadly trap.

With Fate as a Witness

Once the armies were in place, following a frequent custom among ancient military commanders, Caesar and Pompey addressed their respective troops. According to the first century A.D Roman writer Lucan in his epic work *The Civil War*, Caesar said:

> Conquerors of the world, my source of destiny, soldiers! Here is the chance of battle that you have prayed for so often. No more prayers: it is time to summon fate with your swords now. . . . This day will decide, with fate as the witness, which side took up arms with greater justice; the battle fought this coming day will pronounce the guilt of the loser. . . . No nice filial [brotherly] feelings, no softness at seeing your fathers lined up against you. Harden your hearts and slash at their faces. Any soldier who plunges his sword in the heart of a kinsman gets high credit from me for his crime. . . . Say good-bye to your camp, tonight you will sleep in another.[46]

Lucan recorded Pompey as saying to his own men:

> My men, brave men, you have waited long for this day, and now it is here. It can bring us to the end of the Civil War. . . . Whoever among you yearns for his country . . . his happy home and his wife and children and loved ones left behind, he must fight to retrieve them. . . . Ours is the better cause, and the gods will surely support us. They will guide our weapons to Caesar's heart. . . . Now imagine, men,

Servitude for the Future

"Wrong it would be, when the world was dying, to squander regrets on single deaths, and to follow the fate of this man or that man, giving details of who had his body transfixed [run through] by a sword lunge, who was disembowelled [sliced open] and staggered about on his entrails [insides], who took a sword in the throat and drove it out by the force of one last gasp. . . . One man pierced his brother's heart and, to stay undetected in stripping such a close-kindred body, he cut off the head and hurled it out of sight, while another was hacking away at his father, hoping that people would think from his very rage that it could not possibly be his parent. . . . No time to mourn individual victims. This was a battle unique, not sharing the features of other, past defeats. . . . More was lost than lives and the right to existence; for all time ever to come we [Romans] were laid prostrate [rendered helpless]. This battle established permanent servitude [loss of republican institutions] for every age of the future. What did we, we sons and grandsons of Romans who fought there, what did we do to deserve to be born to a tyranny?"

your mothers . . . [and] the aged senators . . . bowing their grey-haired heads in supplication before you . . . [and] Rome herself, in fear of being under a tyrant, coming out to meet you. Imagine the whole population, present and yet to come, addressing jointly their prayers: "Let me die free!" cry those, and the others, "Let me be born free!"[47]

At the conclusion of the speeches, the two generals took their command positions, and for several minutes a heavy and anxious silence hung over the battlefield.

Then came a piercing trumpet blast signaling the charge, and the largest and costliest battle ever fought between two Roman forces began. As the two armies converged on each other, the men in the front lines hurled their spears. Then Caesar's infantrymen drew their swords and crashed headlong into Pompey's front line. Only seconds later, following the prearranged plan, Pompey's huge mass of horsemen smashed their way into the smaller cavalry unit on Caesar's right wing. Pompey's thousands of skirmishers, lightly armored troops utilizing spears, bows, and slings, swarmed in behind his cavalry. Caesar's own horsemen, unable to withstand this huge onslaught, began to fall back.

It was at this moment that Caesar's military genius once more became evident. He had, of course, fully anticipated that his horsemen would have to retreat. As they did so, the foot soldiers he had earlier hidden in the rear suddenly swung around behind Pompey's cavalry unit, trapping it between themselves and Caesar's horsemen. Caesar's men, as he himself described it,

> fell upon Pompey's cavalry with such violence that not one of the enemy stood up to the charge; the whole lot

wheeled around; it was not so much of a retreat as a complete rout in which they galloped off to find safety among the highest hills in the neighborhood. Once the cavalry was out of the way, the [enemy skirmishers], unsupported, abandoned and defenseless, were slaughtered to a man.[48]

With Pompey's left wing obliterated, Caesar's cavalry easily swept around and behind Pompey's infantrymen, who were still slugging it out with Caesar's own legionnaires. As Caesar's forces began to close this second and larger trap, the opposing army panicked and fled from the field. Pompey himself retired to his camp, looking, as Plutarch put it, "like a man

On the bloody field of Pharsalus, Pompey, realizing that the battle is lost, retreats toward his camp.

whom some god had deprived of his wits." It was Pompey's first defeat ever and a humiliating end to a magnificent career. When, soon afterward, Caesar's men began storming the camp, Pompey remarked, "'What, into the camp too?' and, with these words, he took off his general's clothes and, changing into other clothes more suitable for a fugitive, stole away."[49]

A Crippling Blow

As Caesar had promised his men before the battle, many of them slept in the enemy camp that night. Caesar even ate the dinner Pompey's servants had been preparing for their master when they were forced to run for their lives. Regarding Pompey's other followers, some fifteen thousand of his troops lay dead on the gore-strewn plain of Pharsalus and another twenty-four thousand had surrendered. The rest fled into hiding in Greece. By contrast, Caesar had lost only about a thousand men.

With this overwhelming victory, Caesar had accomplished two important goals. First, he had dealt the senatorial forces that Pompey represented a crippling blow from which they would find it difficult to recover. Second, Caesar had gained the personal satisfaction of defeating a man who was recognized as one of the most formidable generals in Rome's history. Yet that defeat would not be complete until Pompey himself was in his hands. Not long after the battle, Caesar learned that Pompey had ridden a horse at top speed to the nearby seacoast and, with a few followers, boarded a grain ship bound for the Greek islands. Caesar could not have known at the time that his opponent would next flee southward to the large island of Cyprus and eventually on to Egypt. There, seeking refuge, Pompey would encounter a grisly fate he had not bargained for. Following hotly on the trail of his one-time son-in-law, Caesar would himself discover an unexpected fate waiting in Egypt. It would be a visit remembered throughout the ages.

5 Fellow Players in the Game of Power: Caesar and Cleopatra

Whether for gold, grain, mystery, or love, Egypt had a way of beckoning Rome's great men. For Pompey, certainly, the choice of Egypt as a place to take refuge after his loss at Pharsalus was calculated rather than random. And Caesar did not go there simply to pursue his defeated enemy. Each man had his own ulterior, or underlying, motive for traveling to Egypt and, seeing himself as Rome's true representative, expected the Egyptians to coop-

This portrait of the Greek general Ptolemy I, founder of Egypt's Ptolemaic dynasty, was copied from a Greek/Egyptian coin.

erate with him fully. But Egypt had unexpected and rude surprises in store for both of Rome's leading figures. Pompey would meet with sudden and brutal death, and Caesar would find himself caught up in the throes of a local civil war. During this crisis, the world's most charming, ambitious, and dangerous woman would attempt to use Caesar to advance her own interests. But as he had done so often in the past, he would find a way to turn such potentially threatening situations to his own advantage. Caesar would draw new strength from his adventures in the Mediterranean world's oldest and, in many ways, most exotic land.

Shelter for Pompey, Money for Caesar

Caesar's and Pompey's motives for going to Egypt derived from the role the country played in Mediterranean politics at the time. In ages past, Egypt had been a great and powerful kingdom ruled by native kings called pharaohs. But over time it had declined and felt the tread of a number of foreign conquerors. One of these had been the Greek king Alexander the Great, who had founded the magnificent city of Alexandria in northern Egypt in the fourth century B.C. After Alexander's death, one of his feuding generals, Ptolemy, had taken control of the country and established a new Greek line of rulers—the Ptolemaic dynasty. Under the Ptolemies Egypt continued to decline until, as a third-rate power, it, like all of its neighbors, had no choice but to recognize Rome's dominance in the Mediterranean. By Caesar's time, Egypt was a Roman vassal state that did whatever was necessary to stay on Rome's good side.

Indeed, it had been to appease Rome that the local ruler, Ptolemy XIII, son of Ptolemy XII, the "Piper," had sent material aid to Pompey while he was building up his forces in Greece. More precisely, Ptolemy's advisors had sent the aid, for at the time the Egyptian king was only thirteen and unable to govern on his own. In Pompey's mind, by giving him its support, Egypt had also given him its allegiance. Now, after the disaster at Pharsalus, he expected the Egyptians to shelter him and provide him with a base of operations from which he might raise new armies to fight Caesar.

Caesar's ulterior motive for going to Egypt was monetary. He needed large sums of money to carry on the civil war, and Egypt's royal treasury was brimming with gold and other valuables. Caesar expected the Egyptians to show allegiance to him, rather than to Pompey, and felt fully justified in demanding a portion of Egypt's wealth. Michael Grant explains:

> When he had been consul in 59 B.C., he and Pompey had agreed to confirm Ptolemy the Piper's title to the throne [then a matter of local dispute] in exchange for huge gifts of money, which

Ptolemy had raised by borrowing from the Roman financier Gaius Rabirius Postumus. When Postumus claimed (no doubt falsely) that his efforts to persuade Ptolemy to repay were unsuccessful, Caesar had personally assumed the responsibility of getting the money back for him—thus providing himself with an excellent excuse for interference [in Egypt] when a suitable opportunity arose. That time had come now.[50]

What Caesar did not count on was that in order to get the money he would have to contend with more than just a boy king and his advisors. Upon his death in 51 B.C., Ptolemy the Piper had left his throne to his son, Ptolemy XIII, and his daughter, Cleopatra VII, who were to rule jointly. Since that time, however, violent court feuds had forced Cleopatra to flee into hiding in the nearby desert. Hearing that Pompey was on his way to Egypt, and reasoning that Caesar would soon follow, Cleopatra, now twenty-one but politically wise far beyond her years, began to draw her plans. Her brother and other adversaries in the court hated and wanted to resist Roman influence. But she accepted the political reality of the day, namely that Rome was undisputed master of the Mediterranean. And she recognized that friendships with powerful Romans like Caesar and Pompey were Egypt's and her own tickets to power and prosperity.

Pompey's Demise

But benefiting from Pompey's friendship soon became impossible for Cleopatra or

his head military commander, Achillas, decided not to help Pompey defy Caesar. Caesar later recorded in his journal:

> It may be . . . that they were really afraid that Pompey might tamper with the loyalty of the royal army and occupy Alexandria and Egypt; or it may be that they regarded his prospects as hopeless and acted according to the common rule by which a man's friends become his enemies in adversity. In any case, they gave what appeared to be a friendly and generous reply to Pompey's messengers and invited him to come and visit the king. Meanwhile they had their own secret plan; they sent Achillas . . . an utterly unscrupulous [dishonest] character, and Lucius Sempronius, a Roman officer, to assassinate Pompey.[51]

Achillas, Sempronius, and their henchmen rowed a small skiff out to meet the ship bearing Pompey and his wife and close supporters. Pompey immediately became suspicious when he saw that neither the king nor any high court dignitaries had come to greet him, as was the custom when men of Pompey's stature visited foreign lands. But he had no reason to expect treachery. So he entered the skiff alone, no doubt intending to send for his wife and the others after he had negotiated with the king. In his *Roman History*, the Roman historian Appian told what happened next:

> While rowing to the shore all were silent, and this made him [Pompey] still more suspicious. Finally . . . recognizing Sempronius as a Roman soldier who had served under him . . . he turned to him and said, "Do I know

This carving from the Egyptian temple at Dendera purportedly depicts Cleopatra wearing the mystic crown of the goddess Isis.

anyone else. While the defeated general was on his way to Egypt, the young king, swayed by his chief advisor, Pothinus, and

you, comrade?" The other nodded and, as Pompey turned away, he immediately gave him the first stab and the others followed his example. Pompey's wife and friends who saw this at a distance cried out and, lifting their hands to heaven, invoked the gods, the avengers of violated faith. Then they sailed away in all haste.[52]

After the grisly deed was done, Achillas had Pompey's head cut off and placed in a basket. He and Pothinus saved it as a gift for Caesar, expecting him to thank them for slaying his great enemy. They hoped that he would then leave, allowing them to continue controlling Egyptian affairs through their manipulation of the young king. But they had badly miscalculated. When Caesar arrived in Egypt four days after the murder, he expressed his outrage that so great a Roman

would be killed in such a cowardly and underhanded manner. "Take it [the head] away, right out of my sight, this horrible object," Caesar is said to have shouted. "What a gift to have sent! You can tell your king that I count it more of an insult to me than to Pompey even."[53] Caesar ordered the murderers openly to beg for Pompey's forgiveness and then to bury his remains with full honors. Further surprising Pothinus and Achillas, Caesar made it clear that he planned to stay in the country until the Egyptians satisfied his monetary demands.

Cleopatra's Little Trick

But to Caesar's own surprise, he had to put his plans on hold in order to deal with a sudden outbreak of violence. He had

Pompey is treacherously murdered as he rides a small boat toward the Egyptian shore. To the killers' surprise, Caesar was angered rather than pleased by the violent deed.

Pompey's Last Rites

Ancient authors left behind a number of conflicting versions about the fate of Pompey's remains after his murder. Appian claimed that a passerby buried the headless body, while Lucan asserted that on orders from Caesar Egyptian officials buried Pompey. In his Life of Pompey, *Plutarch offered this third version of the aftermath of the renowned general's murder:*

"When the people on the ship saw the murder, they gave such a cry that it could be heard from the shore. Then they hurriedly weighed anchor and took to flight. . . . [The murderers] cut off Pompey's head and threw the rest of his body out of the boat, leaving it there as a spectacle for those that desired to see such a sight. Philip [Pompey's servant], however, stayed by the body until they had had their fill of gazing at it. He then washed it in sea water and wrapped it in one of his own tunics. Then . . . he searched up and down the coast until he found some broken planks of a small fishing boat, old and decaying, but enough to make a funeral pyre for a naked and mutilated body. As he was . . . building the pyre, an old man came up who was a Roman and who in his youth had served with Pompey in his first campaigns. 'Who are you,' he said, 'who are preparing the funeral for Pompey the Great?' Philip said that he was Pompey's ex-slave and the old man said: 'But you must not have this honor all to yourself. Let me too share in the pious work. . . . I shall not altogether regret my life in a foreign land if, in return for so many hardships, I find this happiness at last—to touch with my hands and to prepare for burial the body of the greatest commander that Rome has seen.' And so were performed the last rites for Pompey."

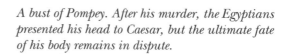

A bust of Pompey. After his murder, the Egyptians presented his head to Caesar, but the ultimate fate of his body remains in dispute.

brought with him only a few ships and troops, but many Egyptians apparently felt threatened. As he and his forces approached the docks in Alexandria, rumors spread among crowds of local soldiers and civilians that Caesar planned to seize the city and overthrow the Ptolemaic monarchy. Caesar later wrote:

> As soon as I landed I was greeted by the angry shouting of the soldiers whom the king had left to garrison [protect] the city, and I saw a great mob rushing toward me. This was because the *fasces* [symbols of Roman power] were being carried in front of me, and the whole crowd considered this to be an infringement of the royal authority. The disturbance was put down, but for several days on end rioting broke out as a result of mass demonstrations and many of my soldiers were killed in all parts of the city.[54]

Caesar soon found that he was, at least for the moment, trapped in this hostile and dangerous city. Strong seasonal northerly winds had begun blowing, and these were enough to keep his ships trapped in Alexandria's harbor. He therefore decided, much to the displeasure of Ptolemy, Pothinus, and Achillas, to take up residence in the royal palace until the situation calmed down. He had no sooner settled into a suite of rooms when he first encountered Cleopatra, who had managed to smuggle herself into the palace, unknown to her enemies. According to Plutarch's famous account of this daring feat:

> Cleopatra, taking only one of her friends with her (Apollodorus the Si-

cilian), embarked in a small boat and landed at the palace [part of which stood on the edge of the Nile River] when it was already getting dark. Since there seemed to be no other way of getting in unobserved, she stretched herself out at full length inside a sleeping bag, and Apollodorus, after tying up the bag, carried it indoors to Caesar. This little trick of Cleopatra's,

A nineteenth-century painting depicts Caesar's surprise as Cleopatra emerges from her hiding place in his bedclothes. Her boldness immediately impressed him.

I Am a Man, Not a Fish

Of the many later literary versions depicting the story of Caesar and Cleopatra, the late nineteenth-century play by British writer George Bernard Shaw is one of the finest. A liberal mix of fact and fiction, this delightful comedy-drama offers a scene set on a seawall located between the royal palace and the Pharos lighthouse. The players are Caesar, Cleopatra, her servant Apollodorus, and Rufio and Britannus, two of Caesar's officers.

BRITANNUS   Caesar: We are cut off. The Egyptians have landed from the west harbor between us and the barricade!

RUFIO (running to see)   Curses! It is true. We are caught like rats in a trap . . . and we cannot get out. . . .

APOLLODORUS   Not get out! Why not? You have ships in the east harbor. . . .

RUFIO (impatiently)   And by what road are we to walk to the galleys, pray? . . .

APOLLODORUS   I will show you. . . . Defend yourselves here until I send you a boat from the galley.

RUFIO   Have you wings, perhaps?

APOLLODORUS   Water wings, soldier. Behold! (He springs into the air and plunges headfirst into the sea.)

CAESAR (wildly excited)   Bravo, bravo! (throwing off his cloak) By Jupiter, I will do that too.

RUFIO (seizing him)   You are mad. You shall not.

CAESAR   Why not? Can I not swim as well as he? . . .

CLEOPATRA   But me! me!! me!!! What is to become of me?

CAESAR   I will carry you on my back . . . like a dolphin. Rufio: when you see me rise to the surface, throw her in. . . .

CLEOPATRA   No, no. NO. I shall be drowned.

BRITANNUS   Caesar: I am a man . . . not a fish. I must have a boat. I cannot swim.

CLEOPATRA   Neither can I.

CAESAR (to Britannus)   Stay here, then, alone, until I recapture the lighthouse: I will not forget you. . . .

BRITANNUS   One last word, Caesar. Do not let yourself be seen in the fashionable part of Alexandria until you have changed your clothes. . . .

CAESAR   Aha! (He plunges into the sea.)

which showed her bold and insolent nature, is said to have been the first thing about her which captivated Caesar, and, as he grew to know her better, he was overcome by her charm.[55]

This idea, that Cleopatra was a seductress who held Caesar and other leading Romans under her spell, was largely invented by Cleopatra's later enemies and then perpetuated by Plutarch and other writers. She and Caesar apparently did become lovers. And soon afterward he decided to help her in her struggle against her brother. But the evidence shows that he used her just as much or more than she used him. Trapped in a hostile situation, he needed an influential ally he could trust, and Cleopatra, with a network of spies in the palace and a segment of the local populace sympathetic to her cause, was the best candidate. Also, Caesar was an astute judge of character. Looking to the future, he must have recognized that Cleopatra would be a more skillful, as well as friendlier and more trustworthy, Roman vassal than Ptolemy and his scheming and shortsighted advisors. It appears, then, that Caesar and Cleopatra shrewdly used each other. And in the process, these fellow players in the game of power became close and intimate friends.

The Battle for Alexandria

Once Caesar agreed to back Cleopatra in her quest for her rightful place on the throne, she no longer kept her presence in the palace a secret. Her brother and his cronies were undoubtedly livid with anger but could do little about it. She was now under the protection of Caesar's personal bodyguards, who watched over her night and day.

Caesar soon raised Ptolemy's ire even further by demanding that he marry his sister and rule with her jointly, just as their father, the Piper, had intended. Ptolemy and Pothinus were duly intimidated by the presence of Caesar's troops in the palace, so they gave in to his demands. However, this was only a ruse, for they secretly planned to destroy both Caesar and Cleopatra. Near the end of 48 B.C., at Pothinus's order, Achillas assembled the Egyptian army, surrounded the palace, and attempted to wrest control of Alexandria from Caesar's troops. Describing these events and those that followed, Caesar wrote in his journal:

> Achillas had an army which in numbers, quality, and military experience was very far from being contemptible [bad]. There were twenty thousand men under arms . . . and all these troops had had long experience in many wars at Alexandria. . . . Confident in these troops of his and contemptuous [scornful] of the small numbers of my own army, Achillas seized Alexandria, except for that part of the town which we already held. In his first attack he tried to break into the palace where I was in residence, but was beaten off by the cohorts which I had posted in the streets. At the same time, fighting broke out in the harbor area.[56]

The fighting in the harbor was unusually fierce as the Egyptians attempted to take control of Caesar's ships. Achillas realized that, if he succeeded in this task, Caesar would be totally cut off from the

A fanciful depiction of the Pharos, showing the towering stone lighthouse that stood on the small island near the mouth of Alexandria's harbor. The well-built structure remained intact until an earthquake finally toppled it in the 1300s, more than fifteen centuries after it was erected.

military supplies these vessels contained. And he would also be incapable of sending for reinforcements. Luckily for Caesar, after several hours of savage fighting his men retained control of the ships and dock area. As a precaution, he then ordered a contingent of men to land on and take charge of the Pharos, a small island near the harbor's mouth. On this island stood the famous Alexandrian lighthouse, a magnificent 445-foot-high stone structure built more than two centuries before by the famed Greek architect Sostratos. The Pharos was the key to controlling maritime traffic moving in and out of the harbor. "The entrance to the harbor," Caesar explained,

is so narrow that those who control Pharos can stop any ship from sailing in. It was because I was afraid of such a contingency that, while the enemy were fully engaged in fighting, I landed troops on Pharos, seized the place, and installed a garrison there. In this way I made sure of being able to receive supplies and reinforcements by sea. I had already sent out to all the neighboring provinces for reinforcements.[57]

Richly Merited Death

While waiting for these reinforcements, Caesar and Cleopatra remained virtual prisoners in the palace, which was still surrounded by Achillas's soldiers. At the same time, Ptolemy and Pothinus were Caesar's own prisoners within the same walls. This bizarre and strained coexistence between the opposing parties went on for almost two months, until violence erupted once again. This time, Cleopatra's younger sister Arsinoe, who apparently believed that neither Ptolemy nor Cleopatra would survive the civil war, slipped out of the palace and joined Achillas. Arsinoe publicly declared herself to be the true ruler of Egypt, and at the same time Pothinus sent secret messages to Achillas urging him to renew his attacks. Caesar managed to catch Pothinus

---

Men of the Egyptian Army

Even in the midst of the chaos and danger Caesar experienced while trapped in the Egyptian palace, he managed, as in Gaul and other lands, to research and write about local customs and traditions, especially those of a military nature. In this excerpt from his Commentaries, *he remarked on the general makeup of the Egyptian army that surrounded him:*

"There were twenty thousand men under arms, most of whom had once served under [Aulus] Gabinius [a Roman leader who had helped Ptolemy the Piper regain his throne during a dynastic feud], but had now grown accustomed to Alexandrian life with all its license [permissiveness]; had forgotten what was meant by discipline and by the name of Rome; and had married native wives, by whom many of them had children. Their numbers were augmented [supplemented] by men gathered together from the bands of pirates and robbers from Syria, the province of Cilicia, and neighboring parts. They had also been joined by a number of convicts and exiles. Moreover, Alexandria offered a perfectly safe way of escape to our own slaves: all they had to do was to give in their names and join the Egyptian army. If any of them was afterward seized upon by his rightful owner, his fellow soldiers would all come together to rescue him. Being all involved in the same sort of guilt, they regarded any violence directed against one of them as a threat to all. It had become a kind of ancient tradition in the Alexandrian army that these troops had the right to demand the execution of the king's favorites, to rob rich men of their property, to make and unmake kings."

This nineteenth-century painting depicts Cleopatra and Caesar sailing up the Nile River on one of her magnificent pleasure barges.

in the act. Finally tired of putting up with the high advisor's dangerous intrigues, the Roman leader ordered "the instant richly merited death of Pothinus," according to Lucan. "The method was hardly drastic enough. The stake [burning], the cross [crucifixion], or mangling by wild beasts—these would have measured up to his evil deeds: but he only died as Pompey had died [by stabbing]."[58]

With Pothinus dead, the terrified boy king probably thought he would be Caesar's next target. However, feeling that the young man could do him no harm, Caesar allowed him to go free. Ptolemy immediately joined Arsinoe and Achillas, and the three began planning a major offensive against Caesar. But it was too late for them

and their cause, for by this time Caesar's reinforcements had begun to arrive in large numbers. In March 47 B.C., near Lake Mareotis, a few miles from Alexandria, Caesar crushed the Egyptian army once and for all. Achillas and Ptolemy were killed, and the young king's body, clad in golden armor that he had hoped would make him invincible, later washed up on the Nile shore. Arsinoe, who had dreamed of possessing a kingdom, survived, but thereafter possessed only what few essentials Caesar allowed her to keep in her jail cell.

On March 27, Caesar entered Alexandria in a triumphant procession. A contingent of citizens stepped forward and, on behalf of the rest of the populace, begged Caesar to forgive them for any past violent acts against him and his men. Now confident that the Alexandrians would no longer give him any trouble, he accepted their apology. He then installed Cleopatra on the throne in a colorful public ceremony. Egyptian tradition required that a queen share power with a male colleague and Caesar, hoping to maintain a peaceful and lucrative relationship with Egypt, wanted to keep the natives happy. So he also installed on the throne Cleopatra's twelve-year-old half-brother, Ptolemy XIV. Since this boy had no powerful advisors, except for the queen herself, Cleopatra was, in reality, the country's sole ruler.

Perhaps because he needed a rest after months of turmoil, and also because he was reluctant to part too soon from Cleopatra, Caesar stayed in Egypt for several more weeks. The queen took him on a luxurious cruise up the Nile, a journey in which they enjoyed numerous sumptuous feasts and visited a number of Egyptian cities. Eventually, however, Caesar felt the pressing need to move on. He had recently learned that Pompey's sons had been reorganizing their father's forces in northern Africa and Spain. And trouble was brewing in Asia Minor, where a local ruler had massacred large numbers of Romans and now threatened the stability of the area.

There was no denying that Caesar's duties as Rome's most powerful figure far outweighed the importance of his relationship with Cleopatra. More political realists than romantics, they both readily accepted this fact. But they parted with the thankful knowledge that they were sure to meet again, for when he sailed from Alexandria in 47, Cleopatra was carrying his child.

6 "I Came, I Saw, I Conquered": Caesar Triumphant

As he departed from Egypt in June 47 B.C., Julius Caesar was nearly fifty-three years old. After more than a decade of almost uninterrupted military campaigns, he felt weary of fighting and was, no doubt, genuinely disappointed at having to carry on the grueling civil war. This strife, he reasoned, should have ended with the showdown at Pharsalus and Pompey's subsequent death. The fact that the war dragged on showed clearly that it was much more than a personal fight between Caesar and Pompey, between the old military guard and the new. It was at its core a mighty death struggle between the crumbling remnants of republican government and the authoritarian forces that were sweeping them away. On the one hand, writes Ernle Bradford, were "the old powerful families, calling themselves the *optimates*, and clinging to the concept of government by the Senate; on the other [hand] Caesar, who envisaged a centralized form of government . . . under a dictator such as himself, with the Senate acting as little more than a rubber stamp."[59]

To ensure that his own vision of government prevailed, Caesar realized, he would have to stamp out the die-hard republican forces gathering against him in the Spanish and African provinces. There,

Pompey's sons, Gnaeus and Sextus, had organized a last-ditch anti-Caesarian resistance. Many senators and former Pompeian officers and legionnaires flocked to their cause, and Caesar fully expected them to raise armies of considerable size and caliber. The challenge would be great, he knew, but, tired or not, there was no other course for him now. As he himself had said, the die had been cast long ago when he had crossed the Rubicon. He had begun the job of creating a new destiny for Rome, and now he must finish it.

To the grim disappointment of his enemies, Caesar would indeed finish the job, and his new vision for Rome would prevail. Two more exhausting years of nonstop campaigning, fighting, and political struggle lay ahead. But at their conclusion he would march triumphantly into Rome as the most powerful national leader in history.

A Campaign Beneath His Dignity

Caesar's informants told him that the republican forces were growing stronger daily. But before focusing his attention on these, his main opponents, he first had to deal with serious trouble in Asia Minor. It was there that the kingdom of Pontus, on the Black Sea, had earlier fought three bloody wars against Rome. Finally defeated in the 60s B.C, Pontus had remained at relative peace ever since, thanks mainly to Pompey's military exploits and authority in the region. But an ambitious local ruler, Pharnaces II, son of Pontus's former king, had recently decided to take advantage of the disorders caused by the Roman civil war. With Pompey eliminated and Caesar seemingly preoccupied in Egypt, Pharnaces attempted to revive his father's kingdom. Boldly determined to drive the Romans completely out of Asia Minor, early in 47 Pharnaces attacked and defeated a small force commanded by one of Caesar's trusted officers, Gnaeus Calvinus. Pharnaces then proceeded to butcher many Roman civilians, going so far as to emasculate, or cut off the sexual organs of, several Roman young men and boys.

Though the civil war was far from over, Caesar already saw himself as Rome's great leader and protector. So he could hardly stand idly by and let Pharnaces' brutal treatment of Roman citizens go unpunished. In the summer of 47, Caesar confronted Pharnaces at Zela, in eastern Asia Minor, where the two armies camped on hills separated by a narrow valley. Before the Romans had even finished erecting their encampment, Pharnaces launched an attack, sending his forces, including war chariots, through the valley and up the opposing hillside. By ordering this mad dash uphill, which clearly gave the enemy the advantage of being able to charge downhill, Pharnaces showed that his military skills were no match for Caesar's. According to the account in the

This later European depiction of Caesar as a triumphant conqueror inaccurately incorporates details from earlier and later periods.

Alexandrian War, a chronicle penned by an unidentified officer on Caesar's staff,

> Caesar was for some time amused by this arrogant display and at the way in which his [Pharnaces'] men were crowded together in a position into which no sane enemy would advance. . . . Caesar was startled by this incredible rashness—or self-confidence. He was caught off guard and unprepared; he was simultaneously calling the troops away from the fortification work, ordering them to arm, deploying the legions and forming the battle lines. . . . While the ranks were still not drawn up . . . royal chariots armed

with scythes [wheel blades] threw them into confusion; however, large numbers of missiles [spears and arrows] were launched at the chariots and they were soon overpowered. . . . The battle cry was raised and they [the armies] came to grips. We were greatly helped by the [downward sloping] nature of the ground.[60]

Thanks to Pharnaces' poor judgment and the superior quality of Caesar's experienced troops, the outcome of the battle of Zela was inevitable. The Romans easily drove the enemy back through the valley and overran their camp. Pharnaces managed to escape but died shortly afterward at the hands of his own rebellious followers. Caesar saw this short campaign as no more than a mere exercise and almost beneath the dignity of a commander who had conquered all of Gaul and bested the great Pompey himself. To emphasize how trivial and easy this latest episode had been, he described it in a letter to a friend in Rome with the brief and now famous phrase *"Veni, Vidi, Vici,"* or "I came, I saw, I conquered."

Caesar and his troops march through Asia Minor on their way to punish Pharnaces II, king of Pontus, for his recent slaughter of local Roman citizens.

Putting Rome's Affairs in Order

Leaving Asia Minor, Caesar arrived in Italy in September 47 B.C. with the intention of organizing his forces for the coming fight against the republicans in Africa. On the road to Rome he met Cicero, who had heard he was coming. Though still a staunch supporter of republican institutions, Cicero correctly foresaw that armed conflict against Caesar was hopeless and would only destroy what little was left of the republic. It would be far better, he reasoned, to cooperate with Caesar for the short term. In time, Caesar would die or somehow fall from power and the Senate might then reassert its former powers. Following this logic, Cicero wisely distanced himself from the Pompeians and offered his support to Caesar, who gladly accepted it.

For now, Cicero's main complaint was that Antony, whom Caesar had left in charge of Rome, would not let the senator into the city. Moreover, Cicero told Caesar, Antony was a poor administrator who had reduced the government to a state of chaos. Caesar found that this charge was true. Antony, who was a heavy drinker and a spendthrift, had spent most of the prior year ignoring his duties and advancing his own career. His worst offense was to take advantage of his high position to speculate on land and houses. Many of Pompey's soldiers and supporters had lost their farms and homes after their defeat at Pharsalus and the government had put them up for sale. Antony grabbed many of these properties, paying far less than they were worth and thereby shortchanging the treasury.

In his usual swift and decisive manner, Caesar put Rome's affairs in order. First, he allowed Cicero to return to the city and resume his influential position. Next, Caesar punished Antony by forcing him to pay the rightful price for the properties he had acquired and also by barring him from public office for a period of two years. Caesar also dealt decisively with a group of about five to six thousand of his former veterans who threatened to mutiny. Incited by bands of Pompey's supporters, who hoped to embarrass Caesar, the soldiers demanded money and lands they claimed Caesar had promised them. Fearing for Caesar's life, some of his friends advised him not to confront the ugly mob of soldiers alone, but he boldly did so. The troops tried to intimidate him into meeting their demands by threatening to quit his service at a time when they knew he desperately needed all the men

A bust of Mark Antony, who unwisely engaged in various acts of political corruption while Caesar was away from Rome.

Abusing Caesar's Authority

Mark Antony's poor administration of Rome in Caesar's absence did not surprise many in the upper classes, who knew well Antony's reputation for heavy drinking, partying, and carousing with prostitutes, actors, and other characters considered socially disreputable. In his Life of Antony, *Plutarch explained how many Romans held Antony in contempt*

"for his naughty life: for they did abhor [hate] his banquets and drunken feasts he made at unreasonable [inappropriate] times, and his extreme wasteful expenses upon vain light huswives [mistresses]; and then in the daytime he would sleep or walk off his drunkenness, thinking to wear away the hangover which he had acquired the night before. In his house they [he and his friends] did nothing but feast, dance, and mask [dress up in costumes]: and himself passed away the time in hearing of foolish plays, and in performing marriages for these players, tumblers, jesters, and such sort of people. . . . It is reported that at the marriage of Hippias, one of his jesters, he drank wine so lustily all night, that the next morning, when he came to plead before [the Assembly], which had sent for him, his being queasy-stomached . . . [and] was forced to lay all up [vomit] before them, into his friend's tunic for want of a basin. . . . Now it grieved [decent] men much to see that Caesar should be out of Italy chasing his enemies, to end this great perilous and dangerous war, and that others in the meantime, abusing his name and authority, should commit such outrageous and insolent [acts]."

he could get. But Caesar deftly called their bluff. According to Appian:

> Contrary to the expectation of all, he replied without hesitation, "I discharge you." Then, to their greater astonishment, and while the silence was most profound, he added, "And I shall give you all that I have promised when I triumph with other soldiers." At this . . . shame immediately took possession of all, [along with] the consideration . . . that while they would be

thought to be abandoning their commander in the midst of so many enemies, others would join in the triumph instead of themselves. . . . [They remained] still more silent and embarrassed, hoping that Caesar would yield and change his mind.[61]

Caesar did not change his mind. He informed the men that they were now civilians, pardoned them for their insubordination, and promised them the land they wanted. Viewing demotion to civilian status as degrading, these proud, battle-hardened veterans begged Caesar to reinstate them. They even offered to submit some of their own number to immediate execution in order to make amends. But Caesar remained resolute and quickly filled the men's vacant positions with new recruits. In this one swift and daring stroke, he crushed the mutiny and thoroughly discouraged any future similar episodes. Now, just as swiftly, he turned his attention to the enemy forces that awaited him on Africa's northern shores.

His Opponents Divided

In December 47 B.C., Caesar crossed to Africa. His forces, numbering about thirty-five thousand infantry and two thousand cavalry, were, numerically speaking, vastly inferior to those of his opponents. Gnaeus and Sextus Pompey had amassed an impressive array of anti-Caesarians, including Afranius and Petreius, whom Caesar had allowed to go free after their surrender to him in Spain; Pompey's father-in-law, the able general Metellus Scipio; Marcus Cato, Caesar's hated senatorial nemesis; and Juba, king of the north African kingdom of Numidia, which bordered Rome's province of Africa in the west. These leaders had combined their forces into a huge army consisting of 80,000 infantry, 15,000 cavalry, and more than 100 war elephants. This represented the greatest single military challenge Caesar had ever faced.

Caesar brilliantly overcame this disadvantage by tricking his opponents into dividing their forces. After avoiding battle for several months, he moved his army to

A portrait of Juba, the Numidian king who joined forces with Caesar's Roman enemies, hoping to benefit politically and financially from Caesar's death. His hope proved a vain one.

the coastal town of Thaspus, in what is now eastern Tunisia. Because the town stood on a narrow isthmus, or strip of land, between the sea and a marshy lake, it appeared as though Caesar had inadvertently trapped himself. His enemies immediately mobilized for what they believed would be certain victory. Metellus Scipio took one contingent of men and elephants to the north side of the isthmus, and Afranius and Juba moved a second unit to the south side, some six miles away. With his opponents thus divided, on April 6, 46, Caesar put his plan into action. At his signal, a small squadron of his ships sailed to the shore area along which Scipio had made his camp. Thinking that the ships were about to land troops, and that they themselves would then be trapped, many of Scipio's men broke ranks and fell into confusion. The anonymous author of the *African War*, possibly the same officer who wrote the *Alexandrian War*, recorded that Caesar

> observed Metellus Scipio's army in frantic movement around the rampart [camp stockade], running here and there in confusion, sometimes withdrawing inside the gates, sometimes coming out in a disorderly and reckless fashion. . . . [Caesar's men urged him] to give the signal without further delay, since the gods were clearly indicating that the victory was destined to be theirs. Caesar still hesitated . . . when suddenly a trumpeter on the right wing . . . began to sound the call to charge. This was taken up by all the cohorts and they began to advance on the enemy. . . . Meanwhile, the slingers and archers on the right wing hurled rapid volleys of missiles at the dense mass of elephants, with the result that the beasts . . . turned round and began to trample down their fellows. . . . So our legions quickly got round the elephants and seized the rampart of the enemy.[62]

Once Caesar had captured Scipio's camp, the Pompeians' whole African operation collapsed. Caesar's troops proceeded to massacre Scipio's men, even those who surrendered, and when the news of this slaughter reached Afranius's and Juba's camp, their troops ran for their lives. In the following few days, Scipio, Petreius, and Juba died fighting, while Caesar ordered Afranius to be executed. Rather than submit to his hated enemy,

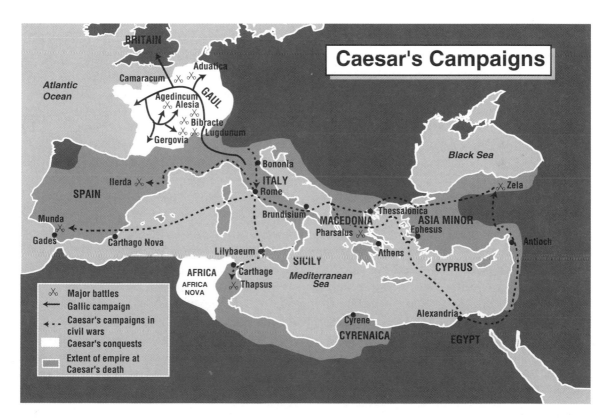

"I Came, I Saw, I Conquered": Caesar Triumphant ■ **79**

Cato committed suicide. The two Pompeys managed to escape and made their way to Spain, hoping to organize still another anti-Caesarian operation. With Juba dead and his forces scattered, Caesar took control of Numidia, which he transformed into the Roman province of New Africa.

The only incident that had marred Caesar's brilliant African campaign was his strange reluctance to order the charge at Thaspus. Plutarch reported that Caesar had not actually fought in the battle, having been afflicted with his "usual distemper." This was a reference to Caesar's epilepsy, the existence of which Suetonius also confirmed. The fact that this nervous system disorder can cause periodic loss of consciousness and/or muscle control may explain why Caesar failed to react at the crucial moment at Thaspus and then did not take part in the battle. Ironically, though the disorder occasionally put him out of action, it may on the whole have worked to his advantage. Besides the "falling sickness," the other ancient name for epilepsy was the "divine malady." A common belief was that a person with the malady had been touched by the gods, or even was himself a god. This seemed to help confirm Caesar's own claim that he was descended from the goddess Venus and thus born to rule over ordinary people.

Rewarding the Troops

The threatened mutiny of one of Caesar's legions, a disaster he managed to head off shortly before leaving for his African campaign, taught him a valuable lesson about making sure that his men were adequately compensated with money and land. In The Army of the Caesars, *Michael Grant comments on some of the measures he took in this regard:*

"It was imperative that the rewards Caesar gave his soldiers should be enough to satisfy their expectations. . . . In 46 B.C. one of his lieutenants, Aulus Hirtius, issued masses of gold coins, of which a great many went to the army. At Caesar's triumphs in 46 and 45 B.C. he gave every infantryman of his veteran legions six thousand *denarii* [common silver coins] as booty. He also inaugurated an extensive scheme of land allotments for discharged soldiers, comprising entire towns in Italy and a number of provinces, together with the territory that went with them. In some of these "colonies of Roman citizens," the soldiers were settled alongside civilians. But at others Caesar settled whole units of his former troops in a single place, scarcely transformed from soldiers at all except that they were now in civilian dress. Like the colonies of Sulla before him, Caesar's were to be bulwarks [strongholds] of his own political support, which was guaranteed by his generous rewards to the settlers."

A Roman cameo depicting Julius Caesar wearing a laurel wreath, in many ancient lands a symbol of victory, honor, and glory.

Caesar's Greatest Honors

In fact, Caesar's ruling image became the first order of business when he returned to Rome in July 46 B.C. With Cato and many other leading senators now dead and republican forces defeated and dispersed, the Senate saw the uselessness of further resistance. Most of the thoroughly intimidated senators now scrambled to appease Caesar, their first move being to appoint him dictator for a ten-year term. They realized that refusing to do so would be pointless, since he would otherwise simply appoint himself dictator. The government also announced forty days of public festivities to celebrate Caesar's victories and erected a magnificent statue of him in a temple on the city's sacred Capitol Hill.

The greatest honors for Caesar were yet to come, however. During all of his campaigns he had never received the triumphs normally accorded victorious commanders, and now he planned to collect these prizes all at once. Between September 20 and October 1, 46, Rome witnessed four huge triumphal parades, one each for his victories in Gaul, Egypt, Pontus, and Africa. "The first and most splendid," wrote Suetonius, "was the Gallic triumph, the next the Alexandrian, then the Pontic [and] after that the African, each differing from the rest in its equipment and display of spoils."[63]

Each triumph consisted of trains of carts and floats bearing captured weapons, jewels, statues, and cabinets loaded with gold and silver, as well as huge paintings depicting the various battles and detailed replicas of notable buildings and whole cities. There were also rows of captured prisoners in chains, dancers, choirs of singers, and entire orchestras of musicians. Each triumph also had a few outstanding featured exhibits which could be counted on to fascinate the thousands of cheering spectators. For instance, Suetonius recorded that in Caesar's

> Pontic triumph he displayed among the showpieces of the procession an inscription of but three words, "I came, I saw, I conquered," not indicating the events of the war, as the others did, but the speed with which it was finished.[64]

The highlight of the Gallic triumph was the chained Arverni chief Vercingetorix, whom Caesar had kept alive in a cell for years, saving him for just such an occasion. Immediately after the conclusion of the parade, having no more use for his prisoner, Caesar ordered the proud Gaul exe-

Caesar's Last War

The battle Caesar fought against Gnaeus and Sextus Pompey at Munda in Spain in 45 B.C. was one of the hardest fought of his career, as reported by Plutarch in this excerpt from his Life of Caesar:

"When all [his] business [in Rome] was over, Caesar . . . set out for Spain against the sons of Pompey. Though they were still young men, they had got together an amazingly large army and showed that they had the daring and courage to command it. In fact they put Caesar into a position of extreme danger. The great battle was fought near the city of Munda. In this battle Caesar, seeing his men being pressed back and making only a feeble resistance, ran through the ranks among the soldiers and shouted out to them: 'Are you not ashamed to take me and hand me over to these boys [Gnaeus and Sextus]?' It was only with great difficulty and after exerting himself to the utmost that he broke the enemy's resistance. He killed over 30,000 of them, but he lost 1,000 of the best troops in his own army. As he was leaving the battlefield he said to his friends that he had often before struggled for victory, but this was the first time that he had had to fight for his life. He won this victory on the day of the feast of Bacchus [Roman god of wine and fertility], the day on which, it is said, four years previously Pompey had set out for the [civil] war. The younger of Pompey's sons [Sextus] escaped, but after a few days the head of the elder [Gnaeus] was brought [before Caesar, who put it on public display]. This was Caesar's last war."

cuted. In a like manner, Cleopatra's sister Arsinoe marched in chains in the Egyptian triumph and the five-year-old son of Numidia's slain king Juba was a featured attraction in the African procession.

Cleopatra herself witnessed the Egyptian triumph after traveling to Rome at Caesar's invitation. He set her up in a beautiful villa on the banks of the Tiber and in all likelihood visited her often. A number of Romans were shocked by what they saw as his scandalous behavior. He was, after all, still married to Calpurnia, a Roman woman of high moral standing. No one had the nerve to express their disapproval publicly, of course, but typical of the private remarks exchanged was that by Cicero in a letter to a friend: "I detest Cleopatra; and . . . I have good [moral] reason to do so."[65]

Another dimension of the scandal was the fact that Cleopatra had brought along her infant child, Caesar's son, whom she had named Caesarion. Trying to defuse the scandal and save face for Caesar, a number of his followers publicly denied that the child was his. His longtime friend Gaius Oppius even published a book claiming Caesar was not the father. However, Caesar himself never denied his paternity. "According to certain Greek writers," declared Suetonius, "this child was very like Caesar in looks and carriage [bearing]. Mark Antony declared to the Senate that Caesar had really acknowledged the boy and that . . . Gaius Oppius and other friends of Caesar knew this."[66]

Cleopatra's likeness carved into a precious stone. Many Romans were shocked when she arrived in Rome with a child she claimed was Caesar's.

Basking in the Light of Power and Glory

For the moment, Caesar seemed to care little what people thought of his morals and private associations. He had never been widely liked personally, except perhaps by his own soldiers, and accepted that a certain amount of scandal and slander was inevitable in politics. Anyway, he was too busy with weighty affairs of state to worry about rumors and gossip. For one thing, he saw the necessity of dealing with the widespread lawlessness that had spread through Rome and other parts of Italy during the recent upheavals of the civil war. Theft, murder, and gang warfare had increased, problems Antony and other recent administrators had done nothing about. To discourage crime, Caesar increased the severity of criminal penalties. He also added a provision allowing the state to confiscate half or more of a criminal's property.

But Caesar wisely recognized that stiffer criminal penalties would not eliminate all social unrest. Part of the problem was that Rome's population had increased sharply in recent years. Thanks to the sluggish war economy, hundreds of thousands of people were out of work. With little else to do but complain and cause trouble, many of the unemployed posed a potential threat to civil order and the state's authority. To deal with the problem, Caesar authorized a large-scale emigration program. He established three new colonies, two on the sites of cities Rome had earlier destroyed—Carthage, in northern Africa, and Corinth, in Greece—and one at Hispalis (later Seville), in southern Spain.

Over eighty thousand jobless Romans immediately emigrated to these new cities, greatly alleviating the crisis of unemployment in the capital.

Caesar had other big social engineering ideas. But to his disappointment he had to put them off for the moment, for the civil war was clearly not over. After escaping the aftermath of the republican disaster at Thaspus, Gnaeus and Sextus Pompey had managed to raise an army of over eighty thousand troops and to seize large portions of Spain. In November 46 B.C. Caesar departed Rome, determined to destroy his enemies once and for all. This he did on March 17, 45, in a savage battle at Munda, in south-central Spain.

With the Pompeians' defeat, grimly highlighted by the death of more than thirty thousand of their number, including Gnaeus Pompey himself, all military resistance to Caesar's rule ended. The dreadful four-year-long ordeal that had pitted Roman brother against brother and son against father was over at last. When he returned to Rome in September 45, Caesar was not only the undisputed master of the Roman world, but quite literally the most powerful human being that had ever lived. Basking in the bright light of supreme power and glory, he could never have guessed that Munda had been his last battle and that in less than six months he would be dead. Though military opposition to him had ceased across the empire, fear, hatred, and jealousy of the dictator remained alive and well in the capital. Caesar's days were numbered.

Chapter

7 The Blood-Soaked Ides of March: Caesar's Last Days

With the civil war over and the empire, at least for the moment, generally at peace, Caesar looked forward to a well-deserved rest from the rigors and dangers of military campaigning. But for the man who was now Rome's supreme dictator, rest did not mean retirement and enjoyment of leisure time. When he returned to Rome from Spain in the autumn of 45 B.C., he immediately began to channel his formidable talents away from securing the empire and into governing it. And he showed remarkable potential as a ruler. In the

brief time he spent in Rome before his untimely death, Caesar proved himself an administrator and civil leader of extraordinary skill, perhaps even of genius. His handling of problems ranging from the national debt to an inaccurate and confusing calendar suggested that he might lead Rome into a bright and constructive future, despite his suppression of many republican freedoms.

But it was Caesar's very disdain for some of the republic's traditional institutions—the Senate in particular—that

The magnificent Capitol, or summit of Rome's ancient Capitoline hill, as it may have appeared in the late first century B.C.

would bring about his downfall. Though the republic was by this time effectively dead, many die-hard republican leaders refused to admit it and desperately sought to bring back the old days. They saw Caesar as standing in the way of what was best for Rome. By contrast, Caesar viewed republican government as outmoded. It involved too many officials and lawmakers, worked too slowly, and as a result got little done. Rome would be better off, he reasoned, with a benevolent dictator, a man who had the empire's best interest at heart and also the power to get things done swiftly and efficiently. Of course, he felt that he was that man.

However, despite their sometimes good intentions, dictators are inevitably grandly ambitious and obsessed with gaining and keeping ultimate power. And Caesar was no exception. Many of the republican leaders admired Caesar's courage, his military skills, and his innovative civil ideas. But they loathed and feared his personal ambition, which was anti-republican and therefore more than enough, in their eyes, to warrant his death. William Shakespeare accurately portrayed their feelings in his play *Julius Caesar*, in which one of Caesar's murderers gives the following justification for the crime:

> Not that I loved Caesar less, but that I loved Rome more. Had you rather that Caesar were living, and die all slaves, than that Caesar were dead, to live all freemen? As Caesar loved me, I weep for him; as he was fortunate, I rejoice at it; as he was valiant, I honor him, but—as he was ambitious, I slew him.[67]

Caesar's Administrative Philosophy

In Caesar's view, Rome needed an ambitious, decisive man like himself to solve some of its pressing social problems. As an example, he pointed with pride to the swift and effective way in which he had recently dealt with the problem of unemployment. Before he had opened up Carthage and the other new colonies to emigration, the government had been regularly handing out free grain to over 320,000 jobless people. This had not only put a strain on state finances, but also given the impression that Roman leaders were incapable of remedying the situation. Late in 45 B.C. his colonization program was only a few months old but already he could confidently announce that it was a success. He had greatly reduced unemployment and at the same time given the government a new, stronger, more decisive image.

This emphasis on innovative programs and speedy, effective government was the foundation of Caesar's administrative philosophy. Most dictators failed, he reasoned, because they used government solely to enrich themselves. A truly benevolent dictator like himself, on the other hand, could succeed by using government to improve people's lives. He sincerely believed that most everyday people would readily give up a few republican freedoms in exchange for useful jobs, financial security, and confidence that the government would meet their needs. In this regard he was right, for most ordinary plebes responded favorably to his social programs. It was mainly the members of the upper classes, particularly the old-style aristocrats

A bust of Caesar as he probably looked shortly before his death in 44 B.C.

noblemen went out to the provinces to take up military commands, these commands were now, with equal completeness, overshadowed by Caesar as commander-in-chief.[68]

Since the members of the ruling class wanted to see Caesar fail, he was not surprised when they grumbled about the success of his colonization program. They grumbled even more at his proposed second step in fighting joblessness and building a new economy. Caesar realized that colonization only helped alleviate unemployment and did not attack the major causes of the problem. One of these causes was the institution of slavery. Most Roman families, except the poorest, had at least one slave, and slaves did most of society's menial labor. That in effect deprived many free Romans of the jobs they needed. In particular, small independent farmers could rarely compete with wealthy aristocrats who owned huge estates that

Roman slaves await sale. Caesar proposed a law (which because of his untimely death was never enacted) greatly reducing the number of slaves.

and politicians who called themselves *optimates*, who opposed his autocratic rule. They did so partly because of nostalgia for the old republican institutions, but also because Caesar, in seizing absolute power, had robbed them of their own. As Michael Grant explains:

> The only men who really objected to Caesar's dictatorial rule were a section, a sizeable section, of the ruling class. For men of this class were devoted to their traditional competition for the leading, senatorial offices of state headed by the annually elected consulships—offices which had formerly carried with them vast and lucrative power. Nowadays, however, although the consulships and other offices still existed, they were totally eclipsed by the dictator: and when the

benefited from the free labor of hundreds or even thousands of slaves. Most of the small farmers ended up on the jobless rolls in Rome and other cities. Caesar did not go so far as to suggest abolishing slavery, which was much too radical and impractical an idea at the time. But he did propose a law that would reduce the number of slaves and require big landholders to fill at least one-third of their work forces with free Romans. This, he held, would not only help to reduce unemployment, but also lessen the danger of slave rebellions like that of Spartacus. Unfortunately, Caesar did not live long enough to put these ambitious and humane reforms into effect, and they died with him.

A Host of Ambitious Projects

In late 46 and early 45 B.C., Caesar began drawing plans for a host of other ambitious and revolutionary projects that he would never see completed. According to Suetonius, for example, he proposed "to open to the public the greatest possible libraries of the Greek and Latin books, assigning Marcus Varro [a prestigious Roman scholar] the charge of procuring and classifying them."[69] Caesar may have gotten this idea from Cleopatra, who had grown up near the magnificent Ptolemaic library in Alexandria, which housed most of the important literary works that then existed. These included original manuscripts by great classical Greek writers such as the playwrights Sophocles and Aristophanes and the philosophers Plato and Aristotle. Whether it was Cleopatra's idea or not, Caesar likely called upon her to lend Varro a staff of Egyptian scholars familiar with running a large library.

Scholars study scrolls in the great library at Alexandria. The modern term "volume" derives from the Greek word volumina, meaning scrolls.

Another idea Caesar may have borrowed from the Egyptian queen was that of building large-scale canals to facilitate and expand trade and commerce. Egyptian engineers were then renowned for building such waterways to irrigate arid regions of their own land. Caesar proposed constructing a canal running from the Tiber River in the vicinity of Rome southward to the Mediterranean shore nearly fifty miles southeast of the city. This would accomplish two purposes, the most important being to increase commerce by allowing ships a second route inland to the capital. Second, while building the canal, workers would drain the Pontine Marshes, a vast swampy area stretching southward from Rome nearly to the seacoast. This would open up much useless land to settlement and farming. Caesar also wanted to build a similar canal near Corinth in Greece to expand Roman trade in that region. In addition, Caesar envisioned making land commerce easier and faster by constructing new roads, some of them hundreds of miles long.

One new project that Caesar did manage to complete, an achievement that has since profoundly affected Western civilization, was a revision of the calendar then in use. In this case, Cleopatra's influence and aid is well documented. As an overseer of Caesar's proposed revision, she recommended the services of the Greek astronomer Sosigenes, who lived and worked in Alexandria. The problem was that the Romans traditionally used the lunar calendar of 355 days, which was more than ten days shorter than the more accurate solar version. "In very ancient times," Plutarch explained,

> there had been great confusion among the Romans with regard to the relation of the lunar to the solar year, with the result that festivals and days of sacrifice gradually got out of place and finally came to be celebrated at the very opposite seasons to what was originally intended. Nor was the confusion confined to the remote past. Even at this [Caesar's] time most people were completely ignorant on these subjects; only the priests knew the proper time, and they, without giving any notice, would suddenly insert in the calendar the intercalary [extra added] month known as Mercedonius.[70]

As long as the priests added this extra month from time to time, the lunar calendar more or less matched the solar one. However, because of the general breakdown of republican government in the first half of the first century B.C., the priests had often neglected to add Mercedonius. As a result, scheduling and coordinating events across the empire had become both cumbersome and frustrating. To clear up this lunar-solar mess, Caesar and Sosigenes introduced a calendar year of 365 days. Because this was still about one-quarter of a day shorter than the actual solar year, they provided for adding an extra day every fourth, or leap, year. This "Julian" calendar became widely accepted thereafter in the Mediterranean world.

Dictator for Life

In the midst of proposing and implementing his political and social innovations, Caesar kept a close eye on the government and the officials who ran it. As he had done with Antony the previous year, he rooted out, then punished or replaced any officials he suspected of corrupt practices. In fact, overall he showed himself to be such a talented, energetic, concerned, and just ruler that even Cicero was amazed. The senator who had for so long criticized Caesar wrote in a letter to a friend that he was "struck with astonishment at Caesar's sobriety [serious attitude], fairness and wisdom. Every day something is done in a spirit of greater clemency [mercy] and liberality [generosity] than we feared would be the case."[71]

Yet not all of Caesar's political moves were as wise and constructive as they might and should have been. In the last few months of his life, he initiated a series of moves designed to further perpetuate his power and to guarantee him one of his fondest goals—everlasting glory after his death. In so doing, he provided his enemies with what appeared to be a justifiable reason for killing him. First, he completely reorganized the Senate, increasing its membership from about six hundred to nine hundred and packing it with his own supporters. It was perfectly clear to all that he was attempting simply to make the legislature agree to any and all of his policies. Moreover, he drew many of the new senators from rural sections of Italy, rather than from urban Rome and its vicinity, as had been the regular custom. The older senators viewed some of their new colleagues as unsophisticated, and others as ill-bred and undignified, as illustrated by Cicero's frustrated remark that the new "men, the Forum and the Senate House are all utterly repulsive to me."[72]

The mood among the older senators darkened further when, in February 44 B.C., Caesar's supporters, at his order, took the bold step of making him dictator *perpetuo*, or "for life." At the same time they heaped other unprecedented honors upon him. "He was proclaimed the Father of his Country," Appian wrote,

> and chosen dictator for life and consul for ten years, and his person was declared sacred and inviolable [untouchable]. It was decreed that he should transact business on a throne of ivory and gold; that he should himself sacrifice always in triumphal costume; that each year the city should celebrate the days on which he had won his victories; that every five years priests . . . should offer up public prayers for his safety; and that the magistrates [government officials] immediately upon their inauguration should take an oath not to oppose any of Caesar's decrees.[73]

A view from one wing of the interior of the Roman Senate House, scene of Caesar's last struggle.

In addition, the state officially changed the name of the year's fifth month, Quintilis, to Julius (July) in his honor. And the state mint issued coins bearing his image and the words "CAESAR DICT PERPETUO," as a further reminder that his dictatorship was permanent.

Then came what Caesar's enemies saw as the most damaging strike against his character and his rule. Rumors began to spread through the capital that the dictator planned to make himself Rome's king. The kingship had been abolished during the establishment of the republic over four centuries before, and most Romans still viewed the concept and very title of king with horror and outrage. Such rumors appeared to have a basis in fact. Cleopatra was still Caesar's lover and confidante, and she, the royal product of a system of absolute monarchy, had openly expressed her disdain for Roman freedoms and republican institutions. Many upper-class Romans had for some time suspected that she was swaying his decisions and pushing him toward absolute rule. Now, in the wake of these new ru-

mors, a real fear grew that Caesar might divorce Calpurnia, declare himself king, and establish a ruling dynasty similar to that of Egypt.

Caesar knew well how much his countrymen hated the title of king. He promptly attempted to quell the rumors. During a public festival in mid February, he had Antony, who was his co-consul for the year 44 B.C., offer him a kingly crown.

We Were Born as Free as Caesar

In his great play Julius Caesar, *William Shakespeare captured well the resentment and animosity the conspirators felt for Caesar in this speech, in which the senator Gaius Cassius tries to convince his colleague Marcus Brutus that Caesar is no better a man than they.*

"I was born as free as Caesar, so were you;
We both have fed as well, and we can both
Endure the winter's cold as well as he.
For once, upon a raw and gusty day,
The troubled Tiber chafing with her shores,
Caesar said to me, 'Dar'st thou, Cassius, now
Leap in with me into this angry flood
And swim to yonder point?' Upon the word,
Accoutered [dressed] as I was, I plunged in
And bade him to follow. So indeed he did. . . .
But ere [before] we could arrive the point proposed,
Caesar cried, 'Help me, Cassius, or I sink!'
I, as Aeneas, our great ancestor,
Did from the flames of Troy upon his shoulder
The old Anchises [Aeneas's father] bear, so from the
    waves of Tiber
Did I the tired Caesar. And this man
Is now become a god, and Cassius is
A wretched creature and must bend his body [bow]
If Caesar carelessly but nod on him. . . .
    Ye gods, it doth amaze me
A man of such a feeble temper should
So get the start of [have first place in] the majestic
    world
And bear the palm [prize of power] alone."

Caesar then made a show of rejecting the offer, hoping that this would prove he had no ambitions to be king. But his enemies remained unconvinced, and a secret and deadly plot began to take shape.

No Alternative

From time to time over the years, a number of senators and other leading Romans had whispered about killing Caesar. But none of the plots against him had ever been substantial or well organized enough to pose him a serious threat. What gave this new conspiracy real substance and urgency was Caesar's sudden announcement that he planned new military conquests in the east. Parthia still remained unpunished for defeating and killing Crassus. And the lands beyond Parthia, the remnants of the former Persian Empire that Alexander the Great had once conquered, beckoned. If Caesar could extend Rome's borders to India, and perhaps even farther, the whole world would come under Roman dominion and he would be remembered as an even greater conqueror than Alexander. He set March 18, 44 B.C., as his departure date for this eastern campaign.

Caesar refuses the crown offered him by Mark Antony during the height of the Lupercalia, the annual public festival celebrated on February 15 in honor of the agricultural god Faunus.

Unmistakable Signs

The Romans, like other ancient peoples, believed in omens, or signs foretelling that something of great importance, either good or bad, was about to happen. After Caesar's murder, a number of legends grew up about omens that had supposedly predicted his death. Suetonius described some of these in his Lives of the Twelve Caesars:

"Now Caesar's approaching murder was foretold to him by unmistakable signs. . . . Shortly before his death, as he was told, the herds of horses which he had dedicated to the river Rubicon when he crossed it, and had let loose without a keeper, stubbornly refused to graze and wept profusely. Again, when he was offering sacrifice, the soothsayer [fortune-teller] Spurinna warned him to beware of danger, which would come not later than the Ides of March; and on the day before the Ides of that month a little bird called the king-bird flew into the Hall of Pompey with a sprig of laurel, pursued by others of various kinds . . . which tore it to pieces in the hall. In fact the very night before his murder he dreampt now he was flying above the clouds, and now that he was clasping the hand of Jupiter [king of the gods]; and his wife Calpurnia [in a dream] thought that the pediment [triangular structure above the door] of their house fell, and that her husband was stabbed in her arms; and on a sudden the door of the room flew open of its own accord."

Caesar's enemies now became angrier and more frustrated than ever. It was bad enough that he had usurped the state's and their own powers and might make himself king at any moment. With his absence in the east, however, their situation would be even worse, for then they would have to do the bidding of his subordinates. The aristocrats deeply resented the idea of following the orders of Balbus, Oppius, and Caesar's other cronies. Most of these were former soldiers and therefore of decidedly lower social status than the ruling class. The thought that in Caesar's absence such men would rule Rome as minor dictators was simply too much to bear.

For Caesar's enemies, there seemed to be no other alternative but to kill him before he left for Parthia.

The great conspiracy was led by the senators Gaius Cassius and Marcus Brutus. At the time, most Romans would never have suspected Brutus to be part of a plot against Caesar. The two men had been friends for years, and there was a real possibility they were father and son, for at about the time of Brutus's birth, his mother had been Caesar's lover. Another of Caesar's longtime friends, Decimus Albinus, his assistant in Gaul, also joined the conspiracy. The reasons these men turned against Caesar remain unclear. Perhaps, as

Marcus Brutus, Caesar's friend, was one of the ringleaders of the assassination plot against the dictator.

the public interest, there would be no danger from Caesar's army.[74]

Death in the Senate

On March 15, known as the Ides of the month, and just three days before Caesar was to leave for the east, the conspirators put their plan into effect. Caesar attended the Senate that afternoon. But Antony accompanied him and it was clear that someone would have to distract Antony to keep him from interfering in the planned attack. According to Plutarch, "Antony, who was a true friend of Caesar's and also a strong man physically, was detained outside the Senate House by Decimus Albinus, who deliberately engaged him in a long conversation."[75]

Once inside the Senate chamber, Caesar walked to his chair while the senators, per custom, all rose in his honor. Then while Cimber pretended to present him a petition, a gang of the conspirators stealthily surrounded him. Suddenly, Cimber grabbed hold of Caesar's toga, which was the prearranged signal to strike, and Casca slashed his dagger at the dictator's throat. The blow missed and wounded Caesar in the chest. At this, Caesar sprang into action and, as Appian described it, "snatched his toga from Cimber, seized Casca's hand, sprang from his chair, turned around, and hurled Casca with great violence."[76] Many of the onlooking senators stood frozen in horror, unsure of whether to intervene or to run from the building.

There was a brief pause, during which Caesar, preparing to fight for his life, took

Shakespeare suggested, they simply revered the Roman Republic more than they loved Caesar. Among the other sixty or so conspirators were the senators Gaius Casca and Tillius Cimber. "When they thought they had a sufficient number," wrote Appian,

> and that it would not be wise to divulge the plot to any more . . . they then sought time and place. Time was pressing because Caesar was to depart on his campaign . . . and then a bodyguard of soldiers would surround him. They chose the Senate as the place, believing that, even though the senators did not know of it beforehand, they would join heartily when they saw the deed. . . . They thought that this deed . . . would seem to be . . . in behalf of the country, and that, being in

a defensive posture. Then, as Casca staggered to his feet, the other conspirators pulled out their own daggers and leaped upon the bleeding man like a pack of wolves. They stabbed him again and again—in the side, the back, the face—spraying blood over themselves and the floor. And all the while, befitting his reputation as a formidable warrior, Caesar valiantly resisted, bellowing in rage and swinging his bare fists. In the confused tangle of thrusting weapons, some of the attackers wounded each other. Finally, his strength ebbing, Caesar collapsed. The assault did not end there, however, for some of the assassins knelt and continued to jab at the twitching body. When they were at last satisfied that their victim was dead, the blood-soaked conspirators ran from the building, screaming "Liberty!"

Caesar's Last Fight

This dramatic description of Caesar's last fight, that with his assassins, comes from Appian's Roman History. *The author based the tract on eyewitness testimony now lost.*

"The conspirators . . . with concealed daggers, stood around Caesar like friends as he sat in his chair. Then one of them, Tillius Cimber, came up in front of him and petitioned him for the recall of his brother, who had been banished. When Caesar answered that the matter must be deferred [put off], Cimber seized hold of his purple robe . . . exclaiming, 'Friends, what are you waiting for?' Then first Casca, who was standing over Caesar's head, drove his dagger at his throat, but swerved and wounded him in the breast. Caesar snatched his toga from Cimber, seized Casca's hand, sprang from his chair, turned around, and hurled Casca with great violence. While he was in this position another one stabbed him with a dagger in the side. . . . Cassius wounded him in the face, Brutus smote him in the thigh, and Bucolianus in the back. With rage and outcries Caesar turned now upon one and now upon another like a wild animal, but, after receiving the wound from Brutus [whom he looked upon as a son] he at last despaired and, veiling himself with his robe, composed himself for death and fell at the foot of Pompey's statue. They continued their attack after he had fallen until he had received 23 wounds. Several of them while thrusting with their swords wounded each other."

The blood-soaked assassins continue to stab at the fallen Caesar, who lies dying at the base of Pompey's statue.

Many of those onlookers who lingered to view the corpse no doubt thought it ironic that the mighty Caesar had fallen at the base of a statue of his one-time nemesis, Pompey. And there was another irony. In all of his violent and dangerous wartime campaigns, Caesar had never suffered a single wound. Yet now, in peacetime and wearing civilian dress, he lay sprawled in a pool of blood. This suggested that Caesar could not escape his own violent past. A larger-than-life figure, he had accomplished much that was admirable, constructive, daring, and certainly brilliant in his turbulent fifty-five years. But he had also pursued power in a relentless and ruthless fashion and in so doing, either directly or indirectly, brought death and misery to millions. Thus, the events of his life and death seemed to confirm the old adage that a person who lives by the sword will inevitably die by the sword. At the height of his power, his enemies had toppled him using the very same tactics of intrigue and violence that he himself had so coldly and expertly employed.

Immortality in Death

The conspirators who murdered Julius Caesar on March 15, 44 B.C., failed miserably in their attempt to destroy him. Though they killed his body, they could not extinguish his spirit, his vision for Rome's future, and his mighty legend. One reason that the republican forces who had opposed Caesar for so long won but a hollow victory was that he was already a legend in life. Despite his patrician background and authoritarian style, many plebes, *populares*, and soldiers saw him as their champion. And his bloody

Slaves carry Caesar's body across the Roman forum. According to the Roman historian Appian, Caesar sustained twenty-three knife wounds.

death unleashed the pent-up distrust and anger they felt for the *optimates* and ruling class.

Another reason the conspirators failed was that the republic they were defending existed more in their minds than in reality. As Caesar had long ago realized, the republic had been dying of mortal wounds ever since the days when Rome's armies began swearing allegiance to generals like Marius and Sulla rather than to the state. The civil wars, the Triumvirate, and Caesar himself had all wrought irreversible changes in the old republican institutions. Caesar's dictatorship had become the glue holding together the pieces of a new authoritarian state. When he died these pieces fell apart. As Ernle Bradford puts it, Caesar's assassination

> unleashed a hurricane that devastated the Roman world. Far from ensuring the triumph of republicanism, the death of Caesar ended the Republic forever. . . . Far from the Senate immediately taking over the government, a panic-stricken fear gripped every member who had not taken part in the plot, while even those who had participated in the murder seemed at a loss once the deed was done. Rome itself was paralyzed.[77]

Cicero's Prediction

As this paralysis wore off, the Roman world, divided between the forces defending Caesar's vision of Rome and those defending the dead republic, plunged into a new and disastrous civil war. After driving the conspirators and their supporters from Italy, Antony soon joined forces with Marcus Lepidus, a powerful general, and Gaius Octavius, known as Octavian. Caesar's grandnephew and adopted son, the eighteen-year-old Octavian appeared at first glance to be the least formidable of

This statue shows Augustus, formerly Octavian, wearing a general's breastplate, which bears embossed figures depicting his recovery of Roman banners from "barbarian" enemies.

the group. Only the canny Cicero seemed to recognize that within this crafty and ambitious boy lurked the powers that would shape Rome's future. In a letter dated April 22, 44 B.C., Cicero wrote to a friend, "What do you think will happen, when this boy comes to Rome, where those who have set us free [the conspirators] cannot live in safety? . . . We [republicans], unless I am much mistaken, shall be crushed."[78]

Cicero's prediction soon became reality. Antony, Octavian, and Lepidus formed the Second Triumvirate in the winter of 43 and, in a purge reminiscent of those of Marius and Sulla, immediately began eliminating their enemies. Cicero, the last great republican remaining in Rome, was first on their hit list, and they hung his head in the city's main square. The triumvirs then proceeded to Greece, where Cassius, Brutus, and their republican diehards had raised an army with which to make their last stand. In the summer of 42, near Philippi, in northern Greece, Caesar's successors crushed these last remnants of the republic. Overcome with anguish and hopelessness, Cassius and Brutus committed suicide.

In the years that followed, the civil war degenerated into a battle for supremacy among the triumvirs themselves. Antony and Octavian first pushed Lepidus aside and then fought each other. As Caesar had done, Antony took Cleopatra as a lover and ally. But the lovers' dreams of ruling Rome together evaporated when Octavian decisively defeated them in a huge sea battle near Actium, in western Greece, in the spring of 31. Antony and Cleopatra fled to Alexandria and soon afterward, with Octavian closing in on them, they took their own lives.

The chaos and destruction of the battle of Actium are captured in this drawing of the event. With the aid of his friend, the military strategist Marcus Agrippa, Octavian won the day.

Octavian was now, as Caesar had once been, the most powerful person on earth. Following his famous uncle's example, he replaced the defunct republic with an autocratic form of government, but unlike Caesar, he encountered no opposition. As F. R. Cowell points out:

Fifteen years after Caesar perished, when peace came again at last to the troubled city of Rome, it was achieved partly because many of the actors in the great drama of [Caesar's] age had died, committed suicide, been killed, or had exhausted themselves and their

Cicero (leaning forward from the litter) is murdered by Antony's henchmen. This brutal deed silenced the last of Rome's great republican voices.

countrymen in the miseries of a civil war too long drawn out. The young men in the rising generation at Rome hardly knew the meaning of political liberty, neither had they any experience of stable, orderly government.[79]

Indeed, after many decades of bloodshed, power struggles, and civil strife, the war-weary Roman people were thankful for the order and stability Octavian's rule brought them. In 27 B.C. he took the title of Imperator Augustus Caesar, "The Great Victor and Ruler." In effect, he was Rome's first emperor, and his reign marked the beginning of what came to be called the Roman Empire. Under the long line of Augustus's successors, each of whom also took the prestigious title of Caesar, Rome continued to expand until it encompassed 3.5 million square miles and more than one hundred million people.

A Formidable Legacy

Although the empire eventually declined and in A.D. 476 itself became defunct, Roman civilization left behind a rich legacy. Over time, the small backward kingdoms that replaced the empire grew into the modern nations of Europe. They retained numerous Roman cultural ideas, especially relating to law and statecraft. They also retained the memory of Caesar's and Augustus's versions of benevolent dictatorship, a concept that many modern rulers, including France's military conqueror and

Octavian, having just been proclaimed Augustus, "the exalted one," is greeted by the cheers and salutes of Roman citizens as he exits the Senate House.

dictator Napoleon Bonaparte, tried to emulate. It also became common for modern military generals to study Caesar's campaigns and battle strategies. Napoleon himself, perhaps the greatest pre-twentieth-century modern general, stated that Caesar's *Commentaries* ought to be a required part of every general's education.

Thus, in a way, even in death Caesar continued to triumph. Despite the efforts of his murderers, their beloved republic disappeared, and Augustus replaced it with a government modeled largely on the kind of supreme dictatorship Caesar had created in the last year of his life. In this way, though Caesar did not live to see his many ambitious plans for Rome go into effect, he left behind a political blueprint that profoundly shaped Rome's future. And through the legacy Rome left Europe, many of his ideas survived into modern times. Finally, in perpetuating and glorifying his name and deeds, history bestowed upon him an honor he had often dreamed of in life—immortality in death.

Notes

Introduction: On a Quest for Ultimate Power

1. William Shakespeare, *Julius Caesar*. New York: Washington Square Press, 1959.
2. George Bernard Shaw, *Caesar and Cleopatra*. Baltimore: Penguin Books, 1951.
3. Suetonius, *Lives of the Twelve Caesars*, translated by J. C. Rolfe. Cambridge, MA: Harvard University Press, 1964.

Chapter 1: A Rising Star in Rome: Caesar's Early Years

4. Ernle Bradford, *Julius Caesar: The Pursuit of Power*. New York: Morrow, 1984.
5. Lily Ross Taylor, *Party Politics in the Age of Caesar*. Berkeley, CA: University of California Press, 1968.
6. Plutarch, *Life of Sulla*, from *Lives of the Noble Grecians and Romans*, excerpted in *Plutarch: Fall of the Roman Republic*, translated by Rex Warner. Baltimore: Penguin Books, 1958.
7. Quoted in Suetonius, *Lives of the Twelve Caesars*.
8. Suetonius, *Lives of the Twelve Caesars*.
9. Plutarch, *Life of Caesar*, in *Fall of the Roman Republic*.
10. Plutarch, *Life of Caesar*.
11. Plutarch, *Life of Caesar*.
12. James Henry Breasted, *Ancient Times: A History of the Early World*. Boston: Ginn, 1944.

Chapter 2: To the Summit of Power: Caesar Wins the Consulship

13. Breasted, *Ancient Times*.
14. Plutarch, *Life of Cicero*, in *Fall of the Roman Republic*.
15. Sallust, *The War With Catiline*, in complete works of *Sallust*, translated by J. C. Rolfe. Cambridge, MA: Harvard University Press, 1965.
16. F. R. Cowell, *Cicero and the Roman Republic*. Baltimore: Penguin Books, 1967.
17. Plutarch, *Life of Pompey*, in *Fall of the Roman Republic*.
18. Cowell, *Cicero and the Roman Republic*.
19. Taylor, *Party Politics in the Age of Caesar*.
20. Suetonius, *Lives of the Twelve Caesars*.
21. Bradford, *Julius Caesar*.
22. Taylor, *Party Politics in the Age of Caesar*.
23. Suetonius, *Lives of the Twelve Caesars*.

Chapter 3: For the Honor and Glory of Caesar: The Conquest of Gaul

24. Taylor, *Party Politics in the Age of Caesar*.
25. Julius Caesar, *Commentaries on the Gallic and Civil Wars*, in *War Commentaries of Caesar*, translated by Rex Warner. New York: New American Library, 1960.
26. Caesar, *Commentaries*.
27. Donald R. Dudley, *The Romans, 850 B.C.–A.D. 337*. New York: Knopf, 1970.
28. Caesar, *Commentaries*.
29. Caesar, *Commentaries*.
30. Caesar, *Commentaries*.
31. Plutarch, *Life of Caesar*.
32. Suetonius, *Lives of the Twelve Caesars*.
33. Plutarch, *Life of Caesar*.
34. Michael Grant, *The Army of the Caesars*. New York: Evans, 1974.
35. Caesar, *Commentaries*.
36. Caesar, *Commentaries*.

Chapter 4: "The Die Is Cast": Civil War Engulfs the Roman World

37. Caesar, *Commentaries*.
38. Caesar, *Commentaries*.
39. Suetonius, *Lives of the Twelve Caesars*.

40. Caesar, *Commentaries.*

41. Cicero, *Letters to Atticus*, translated by E. O. Winstedt. Cambridge, MA: Harvard University Press, 1961.

42. Cicero, *Letters to Atticus.*

43. Caesar, *Commentaries.*

44. Grant, *The Army of the Caesars.*

45. Caesar, *Commentaries.*

46. Lucan, *The Civil War*, translated by P. F. Widdows. Bloomington, IN: Indiana University Press, 1988.

47. Lucan, *The Civil War.*

48. Caesar, *Commentaries.*

49. Plutarch, *Life of Caesar.*

Chapter 5: Fellow Players in the Game of Power: Caesar and Cleopatra

50. Michael Grant, *Caesar.* London: Weidenfeld and Nicolson, 1974.

51. Caesar, *Commentaries.*

52. Appian, *Roman History*, translated by Horace White. Cambridge, MA: Harvard University Press, 1964.

53. Lucan, *The Civil War.*

54. Caesar, *Commentaries.*

55. Plutarch, *Life of Caesar.*

56. Caesar, *Commentaries.*

57. Caesar, *Commentaries.*

58. Lucan, *The Civil War.*

Chapter 6: "I Came, I Saw, I Conquered": Caesar Triumphant

59. Bradford, *Julius Caesar.*

60. Anonymous, *Alexandrian War*, quoted in Grant, *Caesar.*

61. Appian, *Roman History.*

62. Anonymous, *African War*, quoted in Grant, *Caesar.*

63. Suetonius, *Lives of the Twelve Caesars.*

64. Suetonius, *Lives of the Twelve Caesars.*

65. Cicero, *Letters to Atticus.*

66. Suetonius, *Lives of the Twelve Caesars.*

Chapter 7: The Blood-Soaked Ides of March: Caesar's Last Days

67. Shakespeare, *Julius Caesar.*

68. Grant, *The Army of the Caesars.*

69. Suetonius, *Lives of the Twelve Caesars.*

70. Plutarch, *Life of Caesar.*

71. Cicero, *Letters to Atticus.*

72. Cicero, *Letters to Atticus.*

73. Appian, *Roman History.*

74. Appian, *Roman History.*

75. Plutarch, *Life of Caesar.*

76. Appian, *Roman History.*

Epilogue: Immortality in Death

77. Bradford, *Julius Caesar.*

78. Cicero, *Letters to Atticus.*

79. Cowell, *Cicero and the Roman Republic.*

For Further Reading

Julius Caesar, *The Battle for Gaul*, translated by Anne and Peter Wiseman. London: Chatto and Windus, 1980. This recent translation of Caesar's famous journal, *Commentaries on the Gallic Wars*, is contemporary, easy to read, and accompanied by several illustrative drawings and photos.

Lionel Casson, *Daily Life in Ancient Rome*. New York: American Heritage, 1975. A fascinating presentation of how the Romans lived: their homes, streets, entertainment, eating habits, theaters, religion, slaves, marriage customs, government, and more.

Peter David, *Julius Caesar*. New York: Crowell-Collier Press, 1968. A good general synopsis of Caesar's life, written for basic readers.

Anthony Marks and Graham Tingay, *The Romans*. London: Usborne, 1990. A summary of Roman history, life, customs, and military and political figures, including Caesar, written for young people and illustrated with hundreds of beautiful, accurate color drawings.

Don Nardo, *Cleopatra*. San Diego: Lucent, 1994; and *Caesar's Conquest of Gaul*. Lucent, 1995. In what can be considered companion volumes to this biography of Caesar, the author presents the famed leader's campaigns in Gaul and Britain and his relationship with the Egyptian queen in more detail.

Don Nardo, *The Roman Republic* and *The Roman Empire*. San Diego: Lucent, 1994; *Greek and Roman Theater* and *The Punic Wars*. Lucent, 1995. In these concise summaries of Rome's rise to power, its culture and religion, and its eventual decline, the author provides background material and a context for understanding Caesar and the forces that shaped him.

William Shakespeare, *Julius Caesar*. New York: Washington Square Press, 1959. In what remains the greatest political play ever written, Shakespeare chronicles Caesar's last days and assassination in 44 B.C. Although dozens of editions of the play can be found on the market, any of which will do for the text itself, this one contains some valuable introductory background material and useful analysis. The feature films of the play released in 1953 (starring Marlon Brando) and 1970 (starring Charleston Heston) are admirable and both are on videotape.

George Bernard Shaw, *Caesar and Cleopatra*. Baltimore: Penguin Books, 1951. Shaw's witty and entertaining play about Caesar's stay in Egypt and his relationship with Cleopatra was also produced as a movie in 1946 (starring Vivien Leigh and Claude Rains). Look for it on videotape.

Chester G. Starr, *The Ancient Romans*. New York: Oxford University Press, 1971. An easy-to-read general survey of Roman history, with a number of informative sidebars on such subjects as the Etruscans, Roman law, and the Roman army. Also contains many primary source quotations by ancient Roman and Greek writers.

Works Consulted

Appian, *Roman History*, translated by "Horace White. Cambridge, MA: Harvard University Press, 1964. This is an invaluable primary source describing in great detail the late republic, the civil wars, and the exploits of the powerful men, including Caesar, who drove the events of those years.

E. Badian, *Roman Imperialism in the Late Republic*. Ithaca, NY: Cornell University Press, 1968. This scholarly work discusses Roman expansion in the republic's last two centuries, including the takeover of Macedonia and the conquests of Caesar, whom Badian calls "the greatest brigand of them all." The author's overall theme is that the motivating force behind Roman imperialism, as well as the republic in general, was the superior attitude and greed of the patrician ruling class.

Ernle Bradford, *Julius Caesar: The Pursuit of Power*. New York: Morrow, 1984. A fine biography of Caesar by a writer known for his penetrating studies of great historical figures, including Hannibal and Christopher Columbus.

James Henry Breasted, *Ancient Times: A History of the Early World*. Boston: Ginn, 1944. Though somewhat dated, this volume remains one of the best general overviews of the ancient world, well researched, well organized, and clearly written.

Julius Caesar, *The Civil Wars*, translated by A. G. Peskett. Cambridge, MA: Harvard University Press, 1966. One of the most commonly quoted translations of Caesar's own account of his adventures fighting Pompey and other fellow Romans. An invaluable source for studies of both Caesar himself and the last years of the republic.

Julius Caesar, *Commentaries on the Gallic and Civil Wars*, in *War Commentaries of Caesar*, translated by Rex Warner. New York: New American Library, 1960. A fine translation of Caesar's journals, in which he described in detail his famous military exploits.

Cicero, *Letters to Atticus*, translated by E. O. Winstedt. Cambridge, MA: Harvard University Press, 1961. In these letters covering the last few years of his life, the great champion of the republic commented on Roman politics, Caesar and his murderers, and his own dislike of Cleopatra.

Leonard Cottrell, *A Guide to Roman Britain*. New York: Chilton Books, 1966. Cottrell, a well-known writer about ancient times, offers this useful guidebook to Roman archaeological sites and artifacts in the British Isles. Descriptions of Caesar's and Claudius's invasions and their later effects on Britain are included.

F. R. Cowell, *Cicero and the Roman Republic*. Baltimore: Penguin, 1967. A detailed, scholarly, and very interesting analysis of the Roman Republic, with much background material about Roman customs, as well as a thorough discussion of late republican politics based largely on Cicero's surviving letters.

Donald R. Dudley, *The Romans, 850 B.C.–A.D. 337*. New York: Knopf, 1970. A very thoughtful overview of Roman history and culture. Advanced reading.

Major-General J. F. C. Fuller, *Julius Caesar: Man, Soldier, and Tyrant*. New Brunswick, NJ: Rutgers University Press, 1965. Fuller, a noted military historian, delivers a very well-written and thorough biography of Caesar, with plenty of emphasis on the organization of his armies. Advanced reading that will appeal mainly to scholars.

Michael Grant, *Caesar*. London:Weidenfeld and Nicolson, 1974. A fine, easy-to-read general biography by one of the most prolific and respected chroniclers of classical civilization. I strongly recommend these other related books by Grant: *The World of Rome*, New York: New American Library, 1960; *The Founders of the Western World: A History of Greece and Rome*, New York: Charles Scribner's Sons, 1991; and especially *The Army of the Caesars*, New York: M. Evans and Company, 1974, which contains much useful and fascinating information about how Caesar and other Roman commanders organized their armies.

Peter Greenhalgh, *Pompey: The Roman Alexander*. Columbia, MO: University of Missouri Press, 1981. A scholarly study of Pompey's life and accomplishments, including his early relations with Marius, Sulla, Crassus, and Caesar. Advanced reading.

G. B. Harrison, *Julius Caesar in Shakespeare, Shaw, and the Ancients*. New York: Harcourt, Brace, and World, 1960. This extremely useful volume is a grab bag of works by and about Caesar, including Shakespeare's *Julius Caesar*, Shaw's *Caesar and Cleopatra*, Suetonius's *Lives of the Twelve Caesars*, Plutarch's bios of Caesar, Brutus, and Mark Antony (all three from the 1579 Sir Thomas North translation), and excerpts from Cicero's letters and Caesar's own Gallic commentaries. Highly recommended.

Archer Jones, *The Art of War in the Western World*. New York: Oxford University Press, 1987. A thorough study of evolving military weapons, strategies, ideas, and inventions, and the important figures who introduced them. Contains a lengthy and very useful discussion of Caesar's overall Gallic strategy.

Lucan, *The Civil War*, translated by P. F. Widdows. Bloomington, IN: Indiana University Press, 1988. Marcus Annaeus Lucanus, known to history variously as Lucan, Lucain, and Lucano, was a contemporary of the first-century A.D. Roman emperor Nero, who encouraged and supported the author's writing of this long poem about the collapse of the republic. Although the work is not a straightforward history and often features stylized versions of the events, Lucan had access to factual sources now lost, and his presentation is basically accurate.

Plutarch, *Lives of the Noble Grecians and Romans*, excerpted in *Plutarch: Fall of the Roman Republic*, translated by Rex Warner. Baltimore: Penguin Books, 1958. This fine, readable translation of Plutarch includes his biographies of Marius, Sulla, Crassus, Pompey, Caesar, and Cicero. Many of the sources Plutarch used have not survived, so his works preserve much knowledge that would otherwise be lost.

Sallust, complete surviving *Works*, translated by J. C. Rolfe. Cambridge, MA: Harvard University Press, 1965. Sallust was one of the more insightful and honest of the Roman historians and is the most important source for the conspiracy of and war with Catiline in 63 B.C. Sallust's *The War with Catiline* contains a long transcription of Caesar's famous speech calling for leniency against the conspirators, which, because the author was a trusted friend of Caesar's, is thought by modern scholars to be fairly accurate.

Suetonius, *Lives of the Twelve Caesars*, translated by J. C. Rolfe. Cambridge, MA: Harvard University Press, 1964. Besides Plutarch's famous bio of Caesar, this is perhaps the most detailed ancient description of the great general and his exploits.

Lily Ross Taylor, *Party Politics in the Age of Caesar*. Berkeley, CA: University of California Press, 1968. Taylor offers a detailed and thoughtful discussion of the men and institutions of the Roman government in the republic's last years. Includes plenty of material on the dealings and double-dealings of the *populares, optimates,* Cicero, Pompey, Crassus, and of course Caesar.

Zwi Yavetz, *Julius Caesar and His Public Image*. Ithaca, NY: Cornell University Press, 1983. This thorough, extremely detailed, and rather dry study of Caesar is recommended for serious scholars only.

Index

Picture Credits

About the Author

Don Nardo is an award-winning author whose more than seventy books cover a wide range of topics. His titles in the Lucent Encyclopedia of Discovery and Invention include: *Lasers, Gravity, Germs, Vaccines, Animation, Computers,* and *Dinosaurs.* A trained historian and history teacher, Mr. Nardo had produced several historical studies, among them *Braving the New World,* the saga of African Americans in Colonial times; a political trilogy that includes *Democracy, The U.S. Congress,* and *The U.S. Presidency*; and biographies of Thomas Jefferson, Franklin D. Roosevelt, and Charles Darwin. His specialty is the ancient classical world, about which he has written *Life in Ancient Greece, The Roman Empire, The Roman Republic, Greek and Roman Theater, The Punic Wars, The Battle of Marathon, The Trial of Socrates,* and what can be considered companion volumes to this biography of Caesar, *Caesar's Conquest of Gaul* and *Cleopatra.* Mr. Nardo has also written numerous screenplays and teleplays, including work for Warner Brothers and ABC-Television. He lives with his wife, Christine, on Cape Cod, Massachusetts.